HAND TOOL BASICS

Woodworking Tools
& How to Use Them

STEVE BRANAM

POPULAR WOODWORKING BOOKS

CINCINNATI, OHIO

popularwoodworking.com

CONTENTS

4   Introduction

CHAPTER 1
THE TOOLS

6   Workbenches

6   Tools

8   Safety

8   Saw Types

11   Plane Types

CHAPTER 2
SHARPENING

16   Sharpening Fist Fights & Fundamentals

22   Back Preparation

24   Convex Bevel on Oilstones

29   Double-Bevel on Sandpaper

31   Double-Bevel on Waterstones

34   Double-Bevel Jig on Waterstones

39   Hollow Grinding & Honing on Diamond Plate

43   Saw Sharpening

50   Card Scraper Sharpening

CHAPTER 3
STOCK PREPARATION

57   Gauges, Squares & Marking Knives

64   Rough Stock Preparation

69   Rough Sawing Exercise

70   Handplane Fist Fights & Fundamentals

73   Fine Stock Preparation

91   Planing Exercise

95   Tapering

98   Panel Raising

CHAPTER 4
SIMPLE JOINERY

107   Grain & Strength

109   Using The Chisel

121   Edge Joints

127   Bookmatched Joints

129   Coopered Joints

133   Tongue & Groove Joints

137   Rabbets

150   Grooves

157   Dados

162   Half-Lap Joints

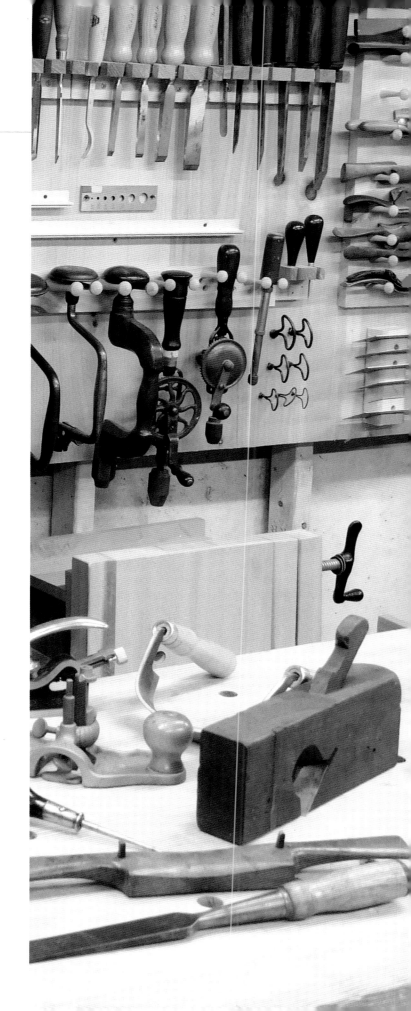

CHAPTER 5

MORTISE & TENON JOINERY

176   Mortise & Tenon Fist Fights &
       Fundamentals

180   Blind Mortise & Tenon

201   Mortise Exercise

202   Tenon Exercises

205   Through Mortise & Tenon

210   Bridal Joint

CHAPTER 6

DOVETAIL JOINERY

215   Dovetail Fist Fights & Fundamentals

218   Through Dovetails

239   Dovetail Sawing Exercise

241   Half-Blind Dovetails

246   Sliding Dovetails

CHAPTER 7

BORING HOLES & CURVED WORK

256   Boring Holes

261   Rounding Out Curves

266   Refining Curves

270   Index

INTRODUCTION

WHY HAND TOOLS?

I'm going to show you how to do all of your woodworking with hand tools. Some may ask, "Why do that when we have power tools available?"

One practical reason that quickly comes to mind is access. If you don't have access to power tools because of lack of money or space constraints (or if you are hesitant to use them because of noise or dust), you can do the same work with hand tools.

There are plenty of other reasons to use hand tools as well, including enjoyment of the craft. Hand tools can be a lot of fun and it is very satisfying to build something entirely with your hands. And even if you don't want to do everything with hand tools, you can incorporate some of these hand techniques into your machine work.

DIFFERENT WAYS OF DOING THINGS

There are a variety of different ways to do things and they have evolved over time. Woodworking has been practiced all over the world, so some methods are regional, some show the influence of specific teachers and schools.

The important thing to remember is that the proven methods all work, even though some of them may seem contrary to one another. Craftsmen have been successful using them in their woodworking for decades.

The methods I show here are based primarily in the English and North American traditions. These are referred to as "Western" style – Asian traditions are referred to as "Eastern" styles. Even among Western styles, there are distinctions between British and continental European styles, just as there are further distinctions among the various Asian styles.

The main differences in these regional styles are reflected in the tools. For instance, Western saws typically work on the push stroke, while Eastern saws work on the pull stroke. There are also differences in techniques.

Everything I'll show you has a long history. There might be some modern variations or versions of the tools, but they all have hundreds of years of history behind them.

Knowing multiple methods allows you to be more versatile. Then you can adapt to different situations based on the tools you have at hand or the particular project that you're working on.

Flexibility is key. You might be able to do 90 percent of a job the same way, but have to vary it for the last little bit. Consistency leads to efficiency, but don't allow yourself to get so set on being consistent that you can't use an alternative method when necessary.

People tend to have very strong feelings about the different ways of doing things, so I'll go over the "fist fights and fundamentals" of woodworking. These are the various arguments about whether to do things one way or another.

I'll outline what the argument is about and break down the fundamentals of the methods to examine why they work. Then you can decide what appeals to you the most and what is appropriate for your tools and situation.

SETTING UP

I use a variety of antique and new hand tools in my work. The specific tools you'll use will likely depend on cost and availability.

The cost to set up a hand tool workshop ranges from $500 to $1,000 to get started. You can always spend more money, but that's enough to get you tools, a sharpening system, a workbench, various workbench appliances and everything you need to do all the basic operations. From there you can go into more specialized tools and your investment will really start to add up.

One of the other interesting things about a hand tool workshop is that you really only need a minimum of a 4'x6' space. That means you can work on a porch, in a spare room, in a corner of a room, under a stair, in a garden shed or in the backyard.

More space is always nice, but you can easily set up a functional hand tool workshop almost anywhere, even if you live in a small apartment.

PRACTICE

Learning to work with hand tools is a lot like learning to play a musical instrument. It takes practice.

Imagine learning how to play the guitar. You have to learn how to tune the guitar, where to put your fingers on the neck to form notes and chords, and how to pick or strum the strings. Then you have to develop the muscle memory to make these skills work.

Your instructor can pour information into your head all day, but until you spend some time practicing, you won't be able to play your instrument.

Similarly with hand tools, you need to put in the time to develop the hand skills. You need to practice and accept that you're going to make a lot of mistakes. Don't worry about it. The best attitude is that there are no mistakes here; there are only learning opportunities.

MATERIALS

For your learning materials, start out with softwoods that are easy to work, such as Eastern white pine. Don't start with the hardwoods immediately. Use something that's relatively soft and is cheap, plentiful and easy to find in your part of the country.

The main advantage of starting with softwoods is that they'll fight you a lot less. You already have plenty of things to deal with in learning how to handle and control the tools, so don't add the wood to that fight.

Later you can move on to hardwoods, like cherry, walnut, maple, oak and mahogany. You'll find that working different kinds of woods generally requires relearning the skills just a little bit, because each wood responds to the tools and techniques somewhat differently.

Lumber straight from the sawmill is called rough-milled. Rough-milled lumber that is then planed on top and bottom is called S2S, for "surfaced 2 sides." This leaves rough edges. S2S lumber that is then trimmed to width on both edges is called S4S, for "surfaced 4 sides."

Lumber must also be dried to a controlled moisture content. It may be air-dried in the open or in sheds for long periods, or kiln-dried in large kilns for short periods (often labeled "KD").

Sawmills and lumberyards typically sell rough-milled, S2S and S4S, both air-dried and KD. Home centers generally only sell S4S KD.

The cost of a given species of lumber depends on how much work has gone into processing it. Rough-milled is the cheapest, followed by S2S and S4S. It's labeled and sold according to its rough-milled thickness and width. Surfacing then reduces those to finished dimensions.

Rough-milled thickness is measured in quarter-inches, such as 4/4, 6/4, and 8/4, for 1", 1½", and 2" material. Planing consumes ¼" and trimming to width generally consumes ½", so when you buy S4S stock labeled as 1"x6", it's actually ¾" thick by 5½" wide. When you buy rough-milled stock, you should expect to remove the same amount of thickness and width yourself.

PHYSICAL WORK

People think that using hand tools is physically difficult and laborious. It's true that you're using your own strength and energy instead of electricity, but part of learning to do this includes learning how to work efficiently and manage your effort.

Some tasks require more physical effort than others. Using hardwoods is harder than using softwoods. But as long as you break up the project into individual parts and steps, no single task is too much work.

Like any other physical activity, pace yourself and take breaks. Don't rush the work.

USING JIGS & GUIDES

You can use commercial, shop-made and improvised jigs and guides for various tasks. Among the many arguments about how to do things, this is a common one.

The arguments in favor of using a guide:

- It allows you better control than you would get freehand.
- It gives you more precise angles, alignment and positioning.
- It allows you to do a task that you are not yet able to do freehand.

The arguments against using a guide:

- If you always rely on it, you'll never develop the skill to work without it; you'll always be dependent on it.
- It's another item to acquire and keep with your tools.
- It adds more things to fiddle with, taking longer to set up.

The strength of these arguments varies by the guide, the job it's used for, and your current skill level. One person's critical tool is another's unnecessary complication.

In some cases, using a guide is a well-established practice. Shooting boards are a good example. They allow you to shoot angles precisely on edges or ends with a plane.

In other cases, the practice is more contentious, with the guide seen as a crutch. For instance, using sawing guides for dovetails, or sharpening jigs for sharpening chisels and plane irons.

The practical approach is to pick the areas where you want to be able to work unguided. Use guides judiciously as required, with an eye toward eliminating them where you want to.

The effort of setting up a guide may add a little time to the work, but working without one may produce unsatisfactory results until you've developed the skill, so set expectations accordingly.

Use guides as a way to develop the skill, not as a replacement for skill. Realize that the learning curve may be long for you to develop some freehand skills. In the meantime, guides allow you to get the work done.

CHAPTER 1

THE TOOLS

WORKBENCHES

The workbench holds your work in place so that you can work faces, edges and ends. Workbenches are equipped with a variety of workholding mechanisms, the vise being the most familiar. However, there are also a number of alternatives to vises.

There are many different designs to choose from, each with its own relative strengths and weaknesses. Costs vary significantly depending on whether you buy one or build it yourself, and what it uses for workholding.

The advantage of a large, heavy workbench is that it will stay in place in use, especially when planing. The biggest problem with lighter workbenches is that they slide around too easily. Lightly built workbenches can also be rickety.

The advantage of a folding workbench is that you can use it in a very small space such as an apartment. Once you're done, fold it up and stand it in a corner. You can also take it with you for off-site work.

A workbench is a compromise of a number of requirements in terms of height, weight, structure, accessories and cost.

TOOLS

The basic tools are handsaws, handplanes and chisels, as well as measuring and marking tools. There are many additional tools for more specialized operations.

You don't need an entire wall full of tools or a large collection to get started. You can start out with a few basics, then add to that as your skills grow.

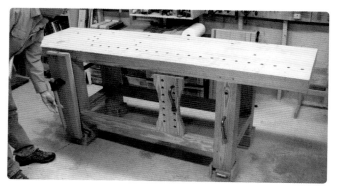

This full-size workbench – about 6' long by 2' deep – has a very thick top and a relatively inexpensive leg vise made from a metal vise screw. Cost for this workbench is about $400 for materials, and $70 for the vise screw.

This bench is smaller, 4' long by 2' deep, but it has a nice quick-release vise mounted on it. The cost of this bench was only about $70 for materials, but $150 for the vise.

This portable folding workbench is 4' long by 2' deep. The cost for this workbench was about $50 for materials.

Another portable folding bench, 4' by 2'. This is a variation of the previous design, with an inexpensive vise. It uses dimensional lumber from a home center. Cost of materials is under $50, and about $20 for the vise.

Modern and antique handsaws.

Left: Three antique wooden-bodied planes. **Right:** Three antique transitional planes.

Modern wooden handplanes.

Left: antique metal-bodied handplanes. **Right:** modern high-quality premium metal-bodied handplanes.

Left to right: antique heavy-duty mortising chisels, lighter-duty modern mortising chisels, fine antique paring chisels, antique socket bench chisels, and modern high-quality premium bench chisels.

Top: antique folding rule. **Middle:** modern wooden marking gauges. **Bottom:** antique combination square, modern marking knife, metal marking gauge and antique engineer's square.

When buying tools, you really have two choices: good quality antique tools that were made at a time when everyone made their living using them, and modern, high-quality premium tools. Avoid cheap modern tools.

Good quality tools, whether old or new, exhibit good design, good materials and good workmanship. While they may be more expensive, they are lifetime investments. Inexpensive modern high-volume mass-produced tools are generally a poor investment – they are often cheaply made using poor-quality materials.

Top: antique brace and bit, eggbeater drill and modern card scraper. **Middle:** antique router plane, small modern router plane. **Bottom:** modern and antique spokeshaves, modern shoulder plane and antique skew rabbet moulding plane.

SAFETY

Hand Tool Safety

Before we use any hand tools, let's take a moment to talk about shop safety. Hand tools are similar in risk to working with kitchen implements. In general they're reasonably safe, but you're working around a lot of sharp edges and teeth. It's not unusual to have little nicks on your fingers, and you're probably going to end up needing a Band-Aid or two.

The one truly dangerous tool is the chisel, because like a large kitchen knife, it's a long, very sharp implement. Safety for the rest of the tools is fairly simple.

Most accidents are due to inattentiveness, improper handling or forcing tools.

Chisels

The safest way to handle a chisel is to always have two hands on it. Have one hand on the handle, the other hand somewhere along the blade. Never point it directly at your body, and never have any part of your body in front of the cutting path, especially your off hand.

You can also choke up on the end of the chisel with your fingers so that they act as a stop, leaving only the tip exposed. That limits how far the chisel can go, useful for working in joints.

A chisel can easily cause very severe cuts, and open up an arm or a hand if you run across its corner.

Be aware of the path the tool may take if something slips or a piece of wood breaks off. Make sure that the exit path is clear no matter what can happen.

Handsaws

Make sure that you're aware of the exit path of the saw. Avoid running the saw across your fingers, especially on the underside of the work.

Handplanes

Handplanes are large enough that you're typically going to have both hands on them. When you're handling them from the underside, always be aware of which way the blade cuts. It's safe to run your fingers from the back toward the front, but not the other direction.

Marking

When you're using a marking knife with a square, make sure that your fingers are not overlapping the straightedge. Make sure they're clear and that you're not going to run your knife over your fingertips.

Marking gauges have sharp points – don't grab the gauge by the points.

Brace & Bit, Drills

Be aware of where the point is going to come out on the opposite side.

Mallet

When using a chisel and mallet, make sure that your thumb and the web of your hand are clear of the top of the chisel. Make sure there's a clear striking area for the mallet.

Dull Tools

Don't use dull tools. If a tool is dull, sharpen it. Dull tools skip across the work, sliding around unpredictably instead of cutting – and they require more force to make them work.

SAW TYPES

Anatomy of a Handsaw

A handsaw consists of the handle and the saw plate. The far end of the toothed edge is called the toe – the near end is the heel.

The shape of a saw handle isn't just decoration, it's ergonomics. This is a highly evolved shape that makes it comfortable to use for long periods, using either a one- or two-handed grip. This gives you control and makes the saw comfortable to use.

Saw handles aren't meant for a full hand, they're meant for three fingers, with the index finger extended along the handle.

This extended finger is very important. I call it the "trigger finger grip." Use this on all your handplanes and saws. It gives you extra control to prevent wobble and maintain a specific angle, especially when using small joinery saws for precision cutting, and using handplanes to plane edges.

Get into the habit of using that trigger finger, even when you're doing rough work that doesn't call for precision – you want it to become second nature. That's one of the main things I have to remind people to do when they're first sawing and planing.

The near end of the cutting edge is the heel, the far end is the toe. The handle is shaped for comfortable extended use.

The trigger finger grip: The hand is cupped around the handle with three fingers and the index finger is extended along the handle.

You have places for your other hand, curling your fingers and hooking your thumb for a two-handed grip.

The horns on the handle provide an alternate gripping position.

Saw Varieties

There are three general types of saws: regular handsaws, smaller joinery saws with backs, known as backsaws, and various framesaws (sometimes also known as bowsaws). Shorter versions of regular handsaws are known as panel saws.

Regular handsaws rely on a thicker plate for stiffness. Backsaws have thinner plates. The back, or spine, provides stiffness. Frame saws have narrow, thin blades that are much more flexible. They provide stiffness by placing the blade under tension, effectively stretching it in the frame.

Top: Crosscut saw. **Bottom:** Ripsaw.

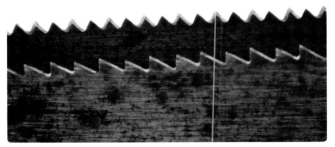

Front: Rip teeth, filed straight across (notice the leading edge is fairly vertical, and the trailing edge is at an angle). **Back:** Crosscut teeth, filed at alternating angles; each alternating tooth has facets that are visible on the leading and trailing edge. The leading edge rakes back, pitching the trailing edge further over.

For all these general types of saws there are two tooth types, determined by function: ripsaws and crosscut saws. Ripsaws are for cutting with the grain (think of ripping a piece of paper lengthwise into strips). Crosscut saws are for cutting across the grain.

The difference is in the way the teeth are filed. Other than that and cosmetic differences, rip and crosscut saws are identical.

For angled cuts, look at how the cut is oriented relative to the grain direction. If the cut is mostly across the grain, use a crosscut saw. Otherwise, use a ripsaw.

There are also various hybrid saws, which have some combination of rip and crosscut teeth.

Rip teeth are the simplest, because they're just filed straight across. Crosscut teeth are more complicated, because instead of being filed straight across, each tooth is filed at an alternating angle.

Both types of teeth are filed with the same triangular file, but it's oriented differently.

The angle at which the leading edge of a tooth is pitched back is called the "rake angle." The alternating angle for filing across crosscut teeth is called the "fleam angle." The bottom space between teeth is called the "gullet." The size of the teeth is called the "pitch" (not to be confused with how the teeth are pitched back).

Rip teeth have very little rake angle, and no fleam angle. Crosscut teeth have up to 30° of rake angle, and up to 20° of fleam angle. Both have gullets that are 60°, the gullet is just oriented differently due to the rake angle.

Sharpening

To sharpen a saw, set the triangular file into a gullet, oriented at the appropriate rake and fleam angles, and file both the leading edge of one tooth and the trailing edge of the tooth in front of it at the same time. Detailed instructions for saw sharpening can be found in Chapter 2.

Because rip teeth are all filed exactly the same, you can hold the file exactly the same way in each gullet. For crosscut teeth, you have to alternate the angle at each gullet.

The easiest way to do this consistently is to first file the odd gullets at one fleam orientation, then file the even gullets at the opposite fleam orientation. This produces the alternating facets on the leading and trailing edges of each tooth.

These filing patterns are what produce the functional differences in the teeth. When ripping, the rip teeth act like little chisels as you push them between the fibers of the wood. When crosscutting, the crosscut teeth act like little knives as you push them across the fibers, severing them. The rip teeth chisel out between the fibers, the crosscut teeth cut across the fibers.

Viewed edge-on, filing a ripsaw straight across. Set the file into a gullet, and file straight across.

Filing a crosscut saw at alternating fleam angles. Set the file into a gullet, and file at the fleam angle.

Saw Pitch

Saw pitch, or tooth pitch, is measured in points per inch (ppi), and it's normally stamped at the heel of the saw. Sometimes a saw may have been re-toothed to a different pitch, so it no longer matches the stamping. Or it may have been resharpened past the stamping, resharpened so many times that the stamped number is gone.

To count the teeth, set a ruler at the point of one tooth, and then count the number of points up to one inch, including that first tooth.

Fine joinery saws are measured exactly the same as larger saws. The only difference is that the teeth are much smaller.

Top: Crosscut saw marked as 8-point. **Bottom:** Ripsaw marked as 6-point.

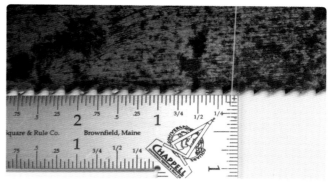

Count the teeth in the first inch, 1, 2, 3, 4, 5, 6. This matches the number stamped on the saw.

A 10 ppi ripsaw, and a 13 ppi crosscut saw. This brand stamps the type of the saw on the back.

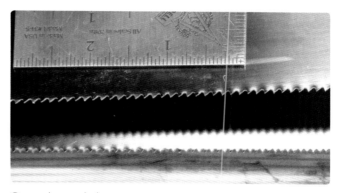

Count the teeth the same way.

PLANE TYPES

Sizes & Numbers

The common metal planes are called "bench planes," because they stay on the bench due to frequent use. The cutters on planes are called "irons."

Different manufacturers use different numbering systems for identifying their planes. The most common is the Stanley system, numbered 1 through 8 for smallest to largest bench plane. These are bevel-down planes, where the iron is mounted in the plane with the bevel facing down. There are also bevel-up planes, where the iron is mounted in the plane with the bevel facing up.

The main question is, which order do you use them in? Do you go from largest to smallest? Smallest to largest? What's the difference?

The difference is that the length of the plane establishes its function. There are three functions for planes, in order of use: roughing, flattening and smoothing. Roughing means removing material quickly. Flattening means making the rough surface flat. Smoothing means getting the final, smooth surface. Flattening may also produce a smooth enough surface that further smoothing isn't necessary, particularly on edges.

Removing material is a rough operation, where you're not concerned yet about getting a flat, smooth surface. This reduces the thickness or width of a piece, getting it roughly to final dimension. Once that step is complete, flattening and smoothing are fine operations, getting the piece precisely to final dimension.

Long planes tend to ride across any high spots in the surface and flatten them out. Short planes tend to ride along the surface, following the contours more than flattening them out. All planes perform some flattening, but the difference in length means that a short plane is much more of a finishing plane, set for a very fine shaving to smooth the surface without appreciably affecting its flatness.

Because of this, long planes are used for flattening, and short planes are used for smoothing. Flattening is known as "jointing" or "trying," so long planes are known as jointers or trying planes. Jointing refers to flattening an edge, while trying refers to flattening a face, and most people use the same plane for both. Short planes are known as "smoothers."

Short numbers 1-4 are considered smoothers. Long numbers 6-8 are considered jointers. One of the factors to help you choose between planes of the same types is your size and strength. For instance, a #7 is heavier and longer than a #6, and a #3 is lighter than a #4.

What about the middle size #5 plane? This is known as a "jack plane." I like to use a jack strictly as a roughing plane, with the iron cambered – or sharpened to a curve. That curve allows the iron to take a deeper shaving, more of a heavy chip that feathers out on the sides. In contrast, the irons for jointers and smoothers are straight across, with the corners rounded or feathered off to avoid leaving plane tracks in the wood.

Therefore, the order of usage is a middle-size jack plane for roughing, a long jointer for flattening, and a short smoother for final smoothing.

Roughing can be very aggressive, taking anything from paper-thick shavings to nearly ⅛" chips, depending on the wood. Flattening is finer, from tissue paper to cardboard thickness. Smoothing is the very finest, from light feathery shaving to tissue paper thickness.

Some people like to use jack planes for everything, from roughing to jointing and smoothing. They may have different irons prepared for each usage. Bevel-up jacks are particularly useful for this.

Anatomy of a Handplane

Most handplanes are comprised of a few key parts including the main body of the plane, the frog (which supports the iron), a handle and knob for gripping, a sole and the iron. The following photos explain the various parts of typical handplanes and how they work.

Left to right: Stanley 7, 6, 5, 4, 3 and 2 planes. The #8 and #1 planes are less practical for general use.

The 3 general sizes in order of use: jack, jointer and smoother.

(A) A bench plane consists of a body, a frog assembly for supporting the iron, a handle, known as a "tote" and a knob.
(B) The bottom side of the body is the bed – or sole – with a mouth for the cutter, known as the iron.

The iron is paired with a chipbreaker, and secured to the frog with a lever cap. The frog has an adjuster knob for adjusting the depth of cut **(A)**, and a lateral adjustment lever for adjusting the angle of the iron across the mouth **(B)**.

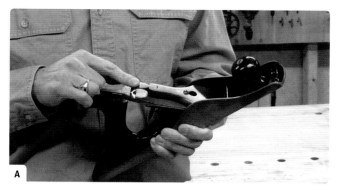

To remove the iron and chipbreaker assembly, lift the lever on the lever cap as shown in photo **A**. Slide the cap off, exposing the iron resting on the frog as shown in photo **B**. Lift that out of the mouth and over the center tensioning screw. This screw allows you to adjust the tension on the lever cap. You should be able to lift the lever of the cap easily, and it should click down in place when you lock it. Turn the screw to tighten or loosen it. Don't overtighten the screw, because that can distort the plane.

(A) The chipbreaker on top of the iron. **(B)** The underside. The purpose of the chipbreaker is to lever chips up and make them curl as you cut. The closer the chipbreaker is to the cutting edge, the finer the chip you can take. To remove the iron from the chipbreaker so you can sharpen it, loosen the screw and slide the hole of the iron over it. Irons get used up over many sharpenings and are replaceable. If you find a nice plane that no longer has a usable iron, you can add an aftermarket iron to it.

To reassemble the chipbreaker and iron after sharpening, lay the iron crosswise over the chipbreaker screw and slide the iron up as shown in photo **A**. Twist it over to align with the chipbreaker as shown in photo **B**, so the chipbreaker edge is behind the iron edge, and tighten the screw hand-tight with a screwdriver. This procedure prevents any contact between the freshly sharpened edge of the iron and metal chipbreaker.

To reinstall the iron and chipbreaker, carefully set the iron into the mouth and over the tensioning screw as shown in photo **A**. The iron rests directly on the frog, bevel down, with the chipbreaker on top. Press the lever cap lever down until it snaps into place as shown in photo **B**. You'll need to adjust the depth and lateral adjustment before using the plane.

Plane Irons

The irons for the different bench planes are shaped slightly differently. Since the #5 is used for roughing, you sharpen its iron to a curve. That's called a cambered iron; it allows you to take a very aggressive cut. Sharpen the other two irons for the #4 and #7 straight across. Then just knock their corners off so that as you make overlapping passes with these planes, they don't leave a track in the wood.

For wooden bench planes, sharpen the irons to the same shapes: cambered for the medium size jack plane, and straight with eased corners for the long jointer and the short smoother.

The #4 iron is straight across. The #5 iron is cambered. The #7 iron is straight across. The corners are rounded off on the #4 and #7 to avoid leaving plane tracks in the wood.

The irons with their chipbreakers, in order of use: #5 jack plane, #7 jointer and #4 smoother. On the #5, the edge of the chipbreaker is about 1/8" back from the edge of the iron. On the #7, it's about 1/32" back. On the #4, it's about 1/64" back.

Wooden Planes

Depending on the task at hand, wooden planes – especially restored or well cared-for antique tools – can be just as effective as metal ones and it's frequently very productive to use both types in the same project. However, because they're constructed quite differently, wooden planes require an entirely different method of adjusting and tuning from their metal counterparts. Often, you'll need to use a wooden mallet to make and set adjustments.

A wooden jack plane. It has a tote, but no knob.

Strike a wooden plane at the back to retract or loosen the iron. This particular plane is a wooden jointer.

You can also strike it on the top front. Some planes have a metal or wooden strike button for this.

Strike a wooden moulding plane at the back the same way. To advance the iron on a wooden bench plane or moulding plane, tap the top of the iron.

Tap the wedge to tighten it up. Always tighten the wedge after adjusting the iron in any way.

The #5 in back is a bevel-down plane. The smaller block planes in front are bevel-up, where the lower bevel angle upward cuts more easily across end grain.

You can mix different plane types, such as this #7 jointer, wooden jack and bevel-up smoother.

Setting planes down on the bench with the toes on a plane strip. That elevates the bottom so that the iron isn't in contact with anything underneath. I prefer this over setting planes on the side, where you might bump another tool into it or bump your hand into the sharp edge.

CHAPTER 2
SHARPENING

SHARPENING FISTFIGHTS & FUNDAMENTALS

There are so many things to argue about when it comes to sharpening edge tools; it's a wonder a riot doesn't break out every time more than three woodworkers get together. Common topics include what kind of abrasive to use, what motion to use, should you use a jig or do it free-hand, how many different levels of abrasive to use and how to shape the bevel.

Woodworkers develop very strong feelings about these things. They split up into different camps, each side questioning the intelligence and character of the other because "only an idiot would do it differently."

A lot of the contention arises because there's no way to measure absolute sharpness. You can't say if a given tool is 50-percent sharp, 90-percent sharp or 100-percent sharp.

There are also a lot of choices. Modern abrasives offer many different methods for sharpening. A variety of jigs are available to aid in the process. Each of these offers various characteristics that some woodworkers like, and some do not.

Which methods appeal to you? As you develop your sharpening skills, you may find that those different characteristics appeal to you differently over time.

Sharpening Steps

Fundamentally, sharpening breaks down into three major steps: grinding, honing and polishing.

As you go through those steps, you go through progressively finer levels of abrasive. You handle the tool in a specific way, moving it across the abrasive to produce a specific angle at the cutting edge of the tool.

Grinding is a coarse step. It removes the bulk of the metal quickly.

Honing is a medium step. It refines the edge, removing very little metal.

Polishing is a fine step. It further refines the edge, removing almost no metal.

Abrasives

The main choices for abrasives include sandpaper on glass, oilstones, various types of waterstones and various types of diamond plates.

There are various sharpening motions for working on these abrasives.

There are also a number of powered alternatives, as well as hand-cranked grinding wheels.

The Sharp Edge

A sharp edge occurs at the intersection of two surfaces. The edge of a plane iron or chisel occurs where the bevel and the back meet.

As the edge is used, it wears down and gets dulled. It gets rounded over. That roundness has a small radius to it. When you sharpen the tool, you're trying to achieve a perfect zero-radius intersection between the two surfaces. Then as you use the tool and wear that edge down, it once again returns to a non-zero radius.

The life of the tool involves sharpening it as close as possible to a zero-radius intersection, using it, wearing it down to a non-zero radius, and then resharpening it for use again – repeating this cycle over and over.

Edge Angle

One of the few things people can agree on is that 30° is a good general-purpose bevel angle at the edge. This angle at the edge of a plane iron or bench chisel is a good compromise between durability and sharpness.

Edges sharpened to a lower angle cut more easily, but they also wear down faster because they're more fragile. Edges sharpened to a higher angle don't cut as easily, but they're more durable.

Therefore, for more specialized tools such as paring chisels, a lower angle is better, down to somewhere between 20° and 25°. For heavier tools such as mortising chisels, a higher angle, up to about 35°, is good.

All of the sharpening methods work for any target angle, not just 30°. Just adjust your setup as necessary for the desired edge angle.

Bevel Profiles

There are three common bevel profiles: double-bevel, convex bevel and hollow-ground. All are sharpened to 30° at the cutting edge. The difference is in how the bevel is shaped up behind the edge.

A double-bevel consists of a primary bevel area at 25°, and a secondary bevel area at 30°. The secondary bevel forms the actual cutting edge.

When you use a double-bevel, you initially grind the entire bevel to the primary bevel angle, 25°. Then you complete it by nipping off the end at the higher 30° angle.

You can resharpen the secondary bevel multiple times before having to restore the primary bevel. Then you can take the primary bevel down near the edge once the secondary bevel gets too large. In this method, the two bevels chase each other back and forth over repeated sharpening. The secondary bevel grows progressively at each sharpening, causing the primary bevel to shrink, then the primary bevel grows, causing the secondary bevel to shrink.

You can also sharpen both the primary and secondary a small amount each time. In this method, the two bevels remain the same relative size at each sharpening.

A microbevel is a form of double-bevel, where the main surface is ground at a primary bevel, and just a very small secondary bevel is added. This secondary microbevel may just be one or two degrees different from the primary bevel.

When you use a convex bevel, you form it all at once every time you sharpen. You always maintain the cutting edge at 30°, while rounding the upper portion of the bevel back behind the edge. At the top of the rounded bevel, the exact angle doesn't matter; it ends up somewhere in the 20° to 25° range.

People get upset by the convex bevel method because they think that you're rounding over the edge. The key point is that you're not rounding over the edge, you're rounding over the trailing portion of the bevel, back behind the edge.

When you hollow-grind, you remove the bulk of the metal on a grinder, then hone and polish on a stone, the same as the other methods.

All of these bevel profiles form the same 30° cutting edge. The only functional difference between them is how you maintain the edges long-term, whether you alternately sharpen and resharpen the primary and secondary bevels, the entire convex face or renew the hollow.

The commonality between all these methods is that they all start off with a rough grinding step to remove the bulk of the metal from the tool. Then you finish them off with finer honing and polishing steps to produce the final edge.

All of these variations of flat, convex and concave surfaces are capable of producing a sharp cutting edge.

Model of the double-bevel. Cutting edge at 30°, 25° behind the edge.

Model of the convex bevel. Cutting edge also at 30°, but curving back to a lower angle behind the edge.

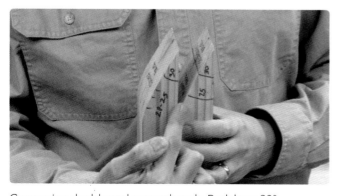

Comparing double and convex bevels. Both have 30° cutting edge.

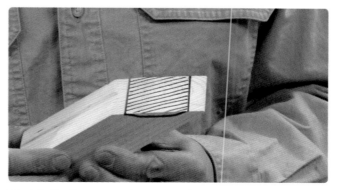

Model of hollow-ground. Cutting edge at 30°, center of bevel hollowed out.

Sharpening Setups

At a minimum, you should have three levels of abrasive for the grinding, honing and polishing steps. A leather strop with stropping compound makes an excellent final polishing step.

The most common types of abrasives are sandpaper adhered to a flat surface, oilstones, various types of waterstones, various types of diamond plates and grinding wheels. The different materials use different grading systems, so it can be difficult to compare the fineness of one with another just by comparing the numbers.

Sandpaper can be used dry, but other methods require some type of lubricant to float the metal particles off the abrasive or cool the metal.

Oilstones use oil, typically mineral or vegetable oil. Waterstones use water. Diamond stones use water or a mild soapy solution, such as dish detergent or glass cleaner. All three types come in both individual grits and combination stones, with one grit on one side, another grit on the other side. Combination stones can be more economical, but you have to flip them in use.

Grinding wheels use water; dunk the metal in the water to cool it. Powered grinders that produce a lot of heat risk burning the temper off the tool if it is not kept cool enough. Hand-cranked grinders are much less likely to cause this.

Waterstones require an extra flattening step. They are meant to abrade away in usage. The muddy slurry is actually an important part of the abrasive action. As a result, waterstones need to be flattened regularly before use, using some other flat abrasive. Diamond plates make good flattening stones.

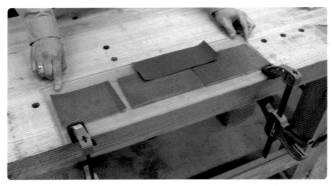

Sandpaper on glass, using a piece of tempered glass bathroom shelving available in the home center shelving section. Coarse, medium and fine grits of sandpaper (#80, #200 and #400). Use self-adhesive paper or adhere it with spray-on adhesive. To finish off, lay three different grits of automotive wet/dry sandpaper (#600, #1,000 and #1,500) loose on top of the sandpaper.

Oilstones, consisting of coarse, medium and fine man-made India stones, a homemade leather strop and a natural translucent Arkansas stone. These are held in a portable sharpening station.

Traditional style pre-soaked Japanese waterstones, in #220, #1,000, #4,000 and #8,000 grits. The #8,000 doesn't need to be soaked. This also includes a coarse diamond plate for flattening the water stones on the left end, and another homemade leather strop on the right end.

Modern style Japanese water stones that don't require soaking, in #1,000 and #10,000 grits, with a coarse diamond sharpening plate for heavy grinding, and a leather strop. On the left is an extra-flat diamond plate used for flattening the waterstones.

Double-sided diamond plates (providing coarse, medium, fine and extra fine, #220, #325, #600 and #1,200) and a leather strop.

A hand-cranked grinding wheel for the rough grinding step using a coarse white wheel. Follow this up with one of the other methods for the honing and polishing steps.

Sharpening Motions

There are several possible sharpening motions on the stones (these also work on sandpaper). Hold the tool at the sharpening angle, then move it in a pattern on the stone. All methods require some practice to maintain proper cutting angle.

The convex bevel method involves the simplest motion: forward and back. It takes advantage of your natural tendency to dip your hand as you push toward the end of the stone. Then you raise the tool back to the cutting angle as you pull your hand back. The repeated strokes dip it, raise it up, dip it and raise it up. This natural motion up and down the length of the stone produces the convex bevel.

Other methods require more control to hold the tool at a specific angle throughout the entire motion. The figure-8 motion is the most complex, involving a lot of wrist and forearm movement.

Work over as much of the stone surface as you can to distribute the wear on the stone. Working too much in one spot risks wearing a low spot.

The tool oriented along the length of the stone. Move it up and down the length of the stone. This is on a diamond plate lubricated with water. Two other motions in this orientation are small circles, working your way over the entire surface of the stone, and figure-8.

The tool oriented across the stone. Hold it at the sharpening angle, then move it sideways up and down the length of the stone.

The tool oriented diagonally between the long and crossways orientations, moved up and down the stone.

Jigs such as this one are meant to eliminate all possible variation in angle as you go up and down the stone.

The Burr & Scratch Pattern

Whichever motion you use, make sure that you're actually reaching the cutting edge. Hold the tool pitched up at the proper angle so that as you hone, you're actually honing at the edge. That's true for both the double-bevel method and the convex bevel method. If you have the tool pitched at too low an angle, you're going to be honing somewhere in the middle of the face, not actually right at the cutting edge.

The way you know that you've crossed the edge is that you'll see a burr developing across it. The burr is a small flap of metal at the edge. It's very thin and flexible. Try to make the burr a uniform size all along the edge.

The scratch pattern on the metal provides a useful way of assessing the effectiveness of each step. As you progress through the grits, the progressively finer grits will produce progressively finer scratches, removing the scratch pattern left by the previous coarser material.

The burr bends back and forth easily. There's no need to produce a larger burr. Once you have a uniform burr across the edge, shift to the next stone.

The scratch pattern produced by the coarse diamond stone.

The polishing stage brings it to a final mirror polish. The back of the tool needs to be equally polished at the end, so that you have two polished faces meeting together to produce that perfect edge.

Stropping

Stropping produces the final polish, taking the edge that last little bit.

You can make a strop by gluing leather down with contact cement onto a piece of plywood sized to match your sharpening stones. Dress the strop with a stropping compound formulated for use with tool steel. This is commonly sold in green or yellow sticks that you scribble onto the leather. There are also materials like diamond paste, which you can use on a bare wood strop without any leather.

Stropping works by two actions. First, stropping on alternate sides fatigues the metal of the burr to break it off. Second, the very fine abrasive action of the compound polishes the surface and removes the microscopic jagged edge left by the burr breaking off.

Some people don't like to use a strop because too much pressure will actually dimple the leather and cause you to round over the edge. You need to use a light to medium pressure so that you're not deforming the leather as you pull the tool across it.

As with the other variables in sharpening, there are people who swear by strops, and there are people who hate them.

Choosing a Setup

All of these setups go through multiple grits to form the entire sharpening process, from the simplest two-grit system of a combination oilstone consisting of a coarse and fine, to three grits of India stones, to four grits of waterstones, to six grits of sandpaper. They all produce some kind of mess, so you have to decide which one you'll put up with.

A very simple and effective setup consists of two stones or sandpapers, in coarse and fine grits and a strop.

Cost ranges from under $100 for a sandpaper system, to about $150 for oilstones and Arkansas stone, to $200 or more for various diamond plates and waterstones. Waterstones require an additional flattening stone, which may add another $50-$200 to your cost.

Sandpaper is the most economical to start with, but it can get used up faster than you might expect, so it adds up over time. Waterstones also get consumed in use, but should last several years. Oilstones tend to be the longest lasting; they can last an entire lifetime.

All of these take approximately the same amount of time to get a sharpening job done. When you've got a well-maintained tool, you don't need to spend more than 30-60 seconds on any particular grit.

You can also mix and match different components of the different methods. You should stick with one bevel type for a given tool, but you can mix different stones or motions. You can also use different methods with different tools. This helps you adapt to the range of different tool shapes, from the tiniest nicker on the side of a wooden moulding plane, to a giant 2" chisel.

Leather strops made from plywood to match the size of the stones. The yellow and green sticks of compound are for polishing steel.

This dull tool is able to shave a little bit off the end grain, but it's producing a poor, crumbly shaving and leaving a rough surface.

This freshly sharpened tool is able to take a continuous feathery shaving and leaves a nicer surface. Scratches left in the surface are a sign of nicks or bits of burr still attached, indicating the edge still needs work.

Conditioning a New Tool

When you have a new tool, whether it's brand new or a used one from the flea market, you may need to condition it to your setup.

This is primarily a grinding process on your coarsest grit, to get it to the proper initial shape.

This can take a little more time than regular maintenance. Tools with damaged edges can take significantly longer, because you have to grind the metal back past the damage.

After that initial grinding, you may need two or three sharpening cycles to get it exactly the way you like it.

Once you're happy with the sharpening that you've established on a tool, the key is to maintain it that way. Don't allow it to get too dull before resharpening it. That's true for handsaws as well as edge tools.

Evaluating the Edge

Because there's no totally objective way to measure sharpness, it's hard to tell when you've done enough honing. You can't tell if it's 75-percent sharp, 90-percent sharp or 100-percent sharp. But there are several subjective ways to evaluate it.

Use caution when checking sharpness. As you become proficient, you'll get an edge that can easily slice flesh and cause severe injury.

A popular method is to see if it will shave the hairs on your arm. However, this has a lot of variability. A better method is if it will slice paper cleanly.

An effective fingernail test is to carefully stand the sharpened edge up on your fingernail and tip the tool backward, pointing the edge away from your finger. If it leans far back before it slides, that means it's a sharp edge. If it slides at a high angle, that means it's dull.

You can also very carefully run your fingernail up and down the sharpened edge. You'll instantly feel any imperfections in the edge. These need further work or they'll leave marks in the wood.

One reasonably objective method is to put some pine in your vise with the end grain facing up and take shavings across it. Pine works well for this because it's so soft. A sharp tool will shear across the end grain cleanly. A dull tool will crush and tear the fibers.

On long grain, a sharp tool should be effortless to use and leave a glassy surface. Once you get a tool to this state, it's great fun to carve off big chunks

with it. This is also good practice for learning how to handle a chisel.

Practice

Each method requires time and practice to master. Get some cheap sacrificial plane irons and chisels and spend some time practicing.

Pick a method and focus on it until you get it down. Even if you decide to switch to another method, you'll find that the experience with one method helps you learn another.

You may even come back to a previous method later on and find that it works a lot better due to your improving skills.

BACK PREPARATION

Back preparation is an important step to make sure that you have two polished surfaces meeting in a sharp edge. The end needs to be a mirror polish on at least the last half inch of the tool. Meanwhile, the entire back needs to be as uniformly flat as you can make it.

Some old tools may have a slight curve or bend in them. This may be pronounced enough that it's not practical to get the entire back uniformly flat. In that case, flatten it as far back from the end as possible. For tools that are straight, it's important to maintain that straightness for the entire back.

While you can do back polishing on your sharpening stones, you can make a simple and effective setup using a variation of the sandpaper and glass sharpening system, using a polished marble or granite floor tile. That preserves your stones for edge work, and ensures that you always have a good flat surface for flattening. Individual tiles are available at home centers for just a few dollars.

Adhere the sandpaper to the tile with spray adhesive. Long and wide strips of regular and wet/dry sandpaper are oriented to allow rubbing the tool alternately sideways and longways. This produces scratch marks in the alternate directions that are easy to see.

A polished marble floor tile on a piece of non-skid padding. It has coarse, medium and fine regular sandpaper (#80-, #200- and #400-grits), and #600-, #1,000- and #1,500-grit wet-dry sandpaper, all adhered with spray-on adhesive.

An alternate setup with the same sandpaper grits, useful for long chisels. Either of these setups should last through several tools before you need to change the paper. You can extend its life by brushing the metal particles out.

1

On the coarsest grit, rub sideways.

2

On the next grit, rub forward and back.

3

Check the scratch pattern to see that the previous marks have been removed.

4

Once the coarser scratch marks have been replaced by the finer marks, continue to the next grit.

5

Continue the process with the wet/dry sandpaper, finishing with the finest grit.

6

The end of the iron is a mirror finish. Further back, it's flat, but doesn't need to be fully polished.

Then you know if you've rubbed the tool enough to remove the previous scratch marks. You can also set up the tile with equal-size strips, regular sandpaper strips on one edge, wet/dry strips along the other edge.

Start with whichever grit matches the condition of the back of the tool. Cheaper tools tend to have coarse grinding and machine marks on the back that require starting on the coarser grits. Higher quality tools have smoother backs, requiring only final polish on the finer grits. For older tools with pitting, you need to decide how much can be cleaned up. You may need to tolerate some pitting left behind, otherwise you would have to grind off large amounts of metal.

If you need to do a lot of grinding on the coarsest grits, be sure to rub the entire back on the sandpaper, not just the end, to maintain overall flatness. Otherwise you risk grinding enough off to take the end out of flat relative to the rest of the length. On the finest grits, this isn't a concern, because you are removing just a tiny amount of metal while polishing.

You only need to bring the end to the final polish. The whole process only takes a few minutes. You'll spend 30-60 seconds on each grit. This back preparation will last for a number of sharpenings. Then polish out the next portion of the back as the tools gets shorter. Over the life of the tool, you'll eventually end up polishing the entire back.

7

Repeat the process when you've flattened back to the end of the polished portion.

8

To change sandpaper, use a single-edge razor blade and a solvent to remove the paper and any trace of adhesive.

CONVEX BEVEL ON OILSTONES

The convex bevel sharpening method is a freehand method that works on any kind of stones. On oilstones, India stones perform the grinding and honing steps. An Arkansas stone and strop perform the polishing step. It takes 20-30 seconds on each stone.

The motion of the tool is forward and back on the stones, starting at 30° and dipping the tool as you move it forward to some lower angle, then raising it back to 30° as you come back.

There are two mistakes to avoid when coming back. First, if you don't come up to 30°, you won't be reaching the edge, so you won't be doing any actual sharpening. Second, if you come up past 30°, you'll be sharpening the edge at a steeper angle than you intended, or worse, rounding over the edge.

For tools that need heavy shaping, for instance those that are a much different bevel profile or have a damaged edge, an extra-extra-coarse diamond stone performs this step. This saves the oilstones for everyday maintenance sharpening. It uses a spray of water or light soapy solution as a lubricant.

Oilstones in a portable sharpening station clamped to the bench. Coarse, medium and fine India stones, strop with yellow compound and translucent Arkansas stone. The wooden angle block in my hand is a sight block cut from a piece of scrap at 30°. Make one for 25° as well.

Extra-extra-coarse diamond stone for heavy shaping, in an auxiliary holder. The holder fits over a stone in the sharpening station to secure it.

Heavy Shaping of a Plane Iron

Let's examine the heavy shaping process as it is used for a plane iron. The steps illustrated below remove a larger amount of metal and get the iron roughly into shape in preparation for sharpening.

1

With the auxiliary holder in the sharpening station and the sight block sitting on the diamond stone, raise the iron parallel to its upper edge. This aligns the iron to 30° at the near end of the stone.

2

Push forward to the far end of the stone. The iron dips down to a lower angle as it moves. Pull back to the starting position. The iron rises back to 30° as it returns.

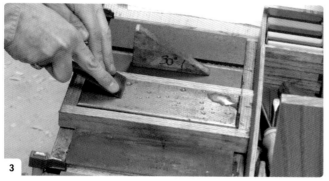

3

Once you have the position, set the block aside and repeat for as many strokes as necessary. This may only take about 20-60 seconds, but grinding back past a damaged edge may take longer. If you need to, realign the iron to the block again.

4

Check for a burr by running your finger forward down the back past the edge. Once a burr has formed along the entire edge, you know that you have actually reached the edge. If the burr isn't complete or the shape isn't ready for sharpening, continue grinding.

Sharpening a Plane Iron

Once you have the heavy shaping out of the way, you are ready to move on to sharpening. For this you'll use oilstones as shown in the following photos.

1

Squirt some oil on the India stones and spread it with the end of the iron held at a low angle. Don't use the edge to spread it.

Don't squirt oil on the Arkansas stone. Just spread some residue from the iron on the Arkansas stone. It's so smooth it doesn't need additional oil. Otherwise when you polish the iron, it will just slide across without actually contacting the stone.

Align the tool to the sight block at the near end of the coarse stone.

Remove the block and move forward and back, dipping the iron as it moves to the far end, raising it back to the 30° as it returns to the near end.

As you go back and forth, move the iron to the left and right to wear the entire surface of the stone evenly. Check the burr to determine when to move to the next stone.

When you're ready to advance to the next stone, pull the iron back to the ready position, lift it and hop it over to the identical position on that stone. If you need to, use the sight block to align the tool again. Repeat the process on the medium, fine and Arkansas stones.

Flip the iron onto its back and lay the end flat on the edge of the Arkansas stone. This is why this stone is at the end position in the sharpening station.

8

Rub the iron up and down the stone to work the burr while holding the iron down flat. You don't need to remove the burr, just flip it up and do a little back polishing.

9

Dress the strop with the stick of compound, scribbling like a crayon. Wipe the oil off the iron and set the bevel down on the far end of strop, angled at 30°. Use the sight block if necessary. With medium pressure, draw the iron toward you along the strop while maintaining the angle. Lift it up to return to the far end, don't push the iron or it will cut into the strop. Do this for 5-10 strokes.

10

Flip the iron onto its back and lay the end flat on the near end of the strop. Draw it toward you while holding it down flat. Do this for 5-10 strokes. Finish up by alternately stropping the bevel and the back one stroke at a time until the burr has completely come off the edge. It may come off in long sections of wire or in smaller pieces, but you should see them left behind on the strop. This leaves the edge polished and razor sharp.

11

If you want to round the corners or feather them off, starting on the coarse stone, tip up the left corner off the stone and put pressure on the right corner. For rounding, work it in small circles. For feathering off, which puts an angled straight segment about ½" wide on the corner, go forward and back.

12

Tip up the right corner off the stone, put pressure on the left corner and repeat the grinding. Repeat these two steps through the grits and strop off any burr that's formed.

13

Examining a feathered iron with a square. The edge is straight across in the center, sloping off at the sides.

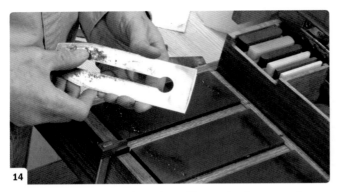

14

For a jack plane, use a cambered iron. The camber is a curve of about an 8" radius on the end of the iron. Do the initial shaping of this curve on a grinder if you can, because it's a lot of metal to remove.

15

To sharpen the camber, treat it as a series of linear segments that approximate the curve, or rock it to the side as you rub forward and back. Apply pressure to the right side as you work it.

16

Apply pressure to the left side as you work it. Since the jack is a roughing plane, this doesn't need to be a perfect curve.

17

Another way to work the curve is to orient the iron across the stone and pivot your wrist side to side. Put pressure on the first trailing side as you pivot one way.

Put pressure on the other trailing side as you pivot the other way.

18

Sharpening a Chisel

The sharpening process for the chisel uses the same set of oilstones and is very much the same as shown for the plane iron. The following photos walk you through the details of the procedure.

1

Set up the chisel parallel to the top edge of the sight block.

Remove the block and do the same strokes as with the plane iron, dipping the chisel as it reaches the far end, raising it back to 30° as it returns to the near end. Repeat for all the grits, 20-30 seconds on each stone.

After polishing the bevel on the Arkansas stone, flip the chisel over to the back, hold it down flat and run the end up and down the side of the stone.

Finish on the strop exactly the same as the plane iron, 5-10 medium pressure strokes on the bevel, 5-10 on the back, then alternating bevel and back until the burr has been removed.

Be sure to avoid rolling the chisel sideways as you work on the stones, in order to keep the edge square across. This is easier for wider chisels.

DOUBLE-BEVEL ON SANDPAPER

This setup uses #80-, #120- and #320-grit self-adhesive sandpaper on a plate of glass shelving from the home center, and #600-, #1,000- and #1,500-grit automotive wet-dry paper. You don't have to match these grits exactly. Sharpening takes 20-30 seconds on each grit.

This uses a side-to-side motion while holding the tool at the bevel angle. Use a 25° sight block to align to the primary bevel angle, and a 30° block to align to the secondary bevel angle. Rock your body back and forth sideways as you maintain uniform pressure on the tool, and don't tip it or change the angle.

When grinding the primary bevel, you don't need to go all the way to the edge and form a burr, because you're going to be working the very end at the secondary bevel. Only the secondary bevel needs to produce a burr.

Narrow chisels are more challenging, because there's so little bearing surface area to keep them flat side-to-side. Concentrate on avoiding rolling sideways as you move back and forth.

Sharpening a Plane Iron

The following photos illustrate the double-bevel sharpening process for a plane iron using sandpaper.

Align the iron to the 25° block on the coarse paper to form the primary bevel.

Align the iron to the 30° block on the coarse paper to form the secondary bevel. Move the iron side the same way. Because the secondary bevel is a relatively small amount of metal to remove, this will be faster than the primary.

Align the iron to the 30° block on the medium paper. Work sideways back and forth for the same amount of time as on the coarse paper. Use the entire surface of the paper.

Move the iron sideways up and down the paper. Check the end to see when the primary bevel is close enough to the end. Realign to the block and continue if necessary.

Run your finger down the back and over the edge to feel for the burr. When it's uniform all along the edge, you're ready to advance.

Maintaining the angle of the iron, hop it over to the fine paper and work it sideways.

Set the wet-dry papers on top of the adhered sandpapers. Align the iron to the 30° block on the coarsest wet-dry.

Advance through the wet-dry papers the same way, hopping from one to the next while holding the angle, about 20 seconds per grit, using the entire surface of the paper.

Flip the iron over onto its back to remove the burr. Holding the end down flat on the edge of the fine sandpaper, work the iron sideways. Advance through the wet-dry grits.

The result is a polished back, with a clean, burr-free edge. This may be sufficient without stropping.

Sharpening a Chisel & a Spokeshave Iron

The process for sharpening a chisel and a spokeshave iron on sandpaper are exactly the same as the process shown for the plane iron. The narrower reference surface of the chisel makes it a little more difficult to avoid rocking the tool. The short spokeshave iron is a little more difficult to hold. Aside from those minor differences, the procedure is the same.

DOUBLE-BEVEL ON WATERSTONES

This setup uses classic style Japanese soak waterstones, in #220-, #1,000-, #4,000- and #8,000-grit, plus a strop. All except the #8,000 need to be soaked for 10-15 minutes before use. The #8,000 just requires wetting with a spray bottle. Sharpening takes 20-30 seconds on each grit.

Waterstones are meant to break down in use, forming a slurry. The grits are much more loosely bound than in oilstones. This also takes the stones out of flat. Waterstones therefore need to be flattened before use. This setup includes a coarse diamond plate as a flattening stone. When flattening, start with the finest stone and work backward through the grits. This ensures that a finer stone isn't contaminated by a bit of coarser grit left

The long primary bevel and narrow secondary bevel on the end of a freshly sharpened spokshave iron.

on its surface. Larger loose grits on a stone will nick the edge of the tool.

In use, spray the stones occasionally to keep a little standing water on the surface. Some people worry about their tools rusting because of the exposure to water, but if you wipe them dry immediately after sharpening, they won't rust.

As with the double-bevel on sandpaper, only the secondary bevel needs to produce a burr.

Sharpening a Plane Iron

Let's examine the double-bevel process for sharpening a plane iron on waterstones.

1

Wet the #8,000 stone with a spray bottle.

2

Press it facedown on the diamond plate and move it in circles to flatten it. It will stick to the plate if you lift it, so slide it off sideways.

3

Repeat this with all the stones down to the #220.

4

On the #220, align the iron to the 25° sight block to form the primary bevel.

5

Locking your elbows at your sides, rock your body forward and back to move the iron while maintaining the angle. Go over the entire surface of the stone to wear it evenly.

6

An alternate orientation is to rotate the iron about 45° after aligning it, then go forward and back. Either way, check the bevel periodically to see when it's near the edge. If necessary, realign to the block and continue grinding.

7

Align the iron to the 30° block, then move the iron forward and back on the #220.

8

Run your finger down the back and over the edge to feel for the burr. When it's uniform all along the edge, you're ready to advance.

9

Advance through the grits. Wipe the previous grit off the iron and realign to the block at each stone.

10

After honing on the #8,000, flip the iron over onto its back to start removing the burr. Holding the end down flat across the side of the #8,000, work the iron up and down the stone. Suction between the flat surfaces will make the iron catch as you move it, so be careful handling it. Wipe the iron dry.

11

After dressing the strop with the stick of compound, hold the iron at 30°, aligning to the block if necessary, and pull it back toward you. Lift and return to the starting position. Repeat for 5-10 strokes.

12

Flip the iron over on its back and pull it toward you while holding it down flat. Repeat for 5-10 strokes. Then alternate bevel and back until no burr remains.

Sharpening a Chisel

The double-bevel process for sharpening a chisel is executed in the same manner.

First align your chisel to the 25° block on the #220 and grind the primary bevel.

Align to the 30° block on the #220 and grind the secondary bevel, checking for the burr. Repeat through the remaining grits.

After honing the bevel on the #8,000, flip the chisel over and hone the back.

Then wipe the chisel off and strop the bevel and back to polish it.

DOUBLE-BEVEL JIG ON WATERSTONES

This setup uses a jig with non-soak Japanese ceramic waterstones in #1,000- and #10,000-grit. The jig can be used with any of the setups, but it always requires a forward and back motion. The main concern in using a jig is to be consistent from one use to the next in setting the angle.

As with pre-soak waterstones, these need to be flattened. This setup uses an extra-flat lapping plate, which is more expensive than a regular diamond plate. It also has a coarse diamond plate for heavy shaping, to avoid excessive wear on the #1,000 waterstone. Sharpening takes 20-30 seconds on each grit.

This particular jig has jaws with wide outer positions for plane irons, and narrow inner positions for chisels. Other jigs have different mechanisms for clamping the tool.

Sharpening a Plane Iron

Let's look at using a double-bevel jig to sharpen our plane iron. The following photos illustrate the procedure.

1. Align the iron in the jig to the 25° sight block.

2. Spray the stones with water. Repeat as needed to keep them moist.

3. Flatten the #10,000 stone first, moving it in circles on the flattening plate.

4. Flatten the #1,000 stone next. It's good to have a bucket for rinsing the stones and plate. You can also leave the slurry on the stones.

5. With the jig and iron on the coarse diamond plate, hook your thumbs behind the upper part of the iron. This plate also uses a spray of water.

6. Place your fingers at the corners on the end of the iron and using medium pressure, roll the jig and iron forward and back until you've shaped the primary bevel. Don't roll off the back edge.

Realign the iron to the 30° sight block.

Tighten the jig snugly with a screwdriver.

Grind the secondary bevel the same as the primary.

Run your finger down the back and over the edge to check for the burr. When it's uniform across the edge, advance to the #1,000 stone.

Roll the jig and iron forward and back.

Wipe the iron off, then advance to the #10,000 stone.

Flip the iron over onto its back to start removing the burr. Run it up and and down the edge of the stone. Wipe the iron dry.

14

With the iron still in the jig, strop the bevel for 5-10 strokes, tipping up on the jig's roller to push forward so you don't cut into the strop.

15

Remove the iron from the jig and strop the back for 5-10 strokes. If any burr remains, alternately strop the bevel and back.

16

The single wheel roller on this style of jig makes it easy to feather off the corners of an iron, because it acts as a pivot point.

17

Put pressure on the first corner and roll forward and back on the #1,000 stone. The jig tips over on the roller.

18

Put pressure on the second corner and go forward and back. Repeat these steps on the #10,000 stone and repeat on the strop.

19

Work the burr on the back.

Tip to each side on the strop, then remove the iron from the jig and strop the back.

20

Sharpening a Chisel

Now, let's examine using the double-bevel jig to sharpen a chisel.

1

Align the chisel to the 25° sight block.

2

On the diamond stone, go back and forth to grind the primary bevel. Once burr has been formed, reset the chisel to the 30° sight block.

3

Hone the chisel on the #1,000 and #10,000 stones.

4

Flip it on its back and hone the back.

5

Strop the bevel.

6

Remove the chisel from the jig and strop the back.

Setting Guide

You can make a simple guide for setting plane irons and chisels consistently in the jig. The jig conveniently has the projection distances for setting tools to 25° and 30° listed on its side. The setting guide is a specialized bench hook with stop blocks at these distances. This type of guide works with other jigs as well, they just use different distances.

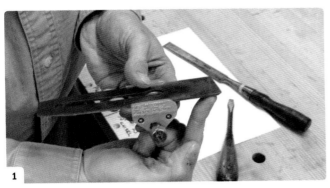

1

The distance that the tool end projects in the jig determines the bevel angle.

2

The setting guide with stop blocks at the correct distances for plane irons and chisels for 25° and 30° bevels.

3

With a plane iron in the outer position of the jaws, butt the end of the iron against the stop block and slide the jig up against the setting guide. Tighten the jig with a screwdriver.

4

With a chisel in the inner position of the jaws, butt the end of the chisel against the stop block and slide the jig up against the setting guide. Tighten the jig with a screwdriver.

HOLLOW GRINDING & HONING ON DIAMOND PLATE

Hollow grinding removes the bulk of the metal from the center of the bevel, leaving just a small amount of metal to be removed by honing and polishing on a fine sharpening stone and a strop. It also provides self-jigging reference surfaces for registering the tool on the stones.

You need to have a good tool rest on your grinder. Most tool rests that come with grinders are very poor. You can buy a commercial aftermarket tool rest or make one. There are a number of different designs.

The main risk with a grinder is overheating the tool and burning the end, drawing its temper. If the metal turns blue or black, it will be brittle. You'll need to grind down past this to get back to good metal.

To avoid overheating, dip the tool in water or spray it to cool it. A hand-cranked grinder runs much slower than a powered grinder, so is less likely to burn the tool.

Depending on how much metal you remove when honing, you may be able to sharpen several times before you have to re-grind the hollow in a tool.

Hand-cranked grinder for grinding, double-sided diamond plates for honing, strop between them for polishing, and spray bottle for cooling the tool.

Krenov-style shop-made tool rest. The clamp secures it to the the plywood base.

Playing cards under the back edge shim the rest to fine-tune the angle.

Set the angle so that when you slide a tool up along the rest, it contacts the stone at 30°.

Sharpening a Chisel

Let's look at the process for sharpening a chisel by hollow-grinding using a hand-cranked grinder and then honing on a diamond plate.

1 Set the chisel on the rest just in contact with the wheel. Crank the wheel as you slide the tool sideways. This requires a careful grinding job. Spray the tool end to cool it.

2 The two flat areas left after hollow-grinding the center of the bevel, highlighted with black marker for visibility. These flats provide the self-jigging action.

3

Spray the extra-fine diamond plate with water. Because there is so little metal to remove, this grit is the only one needed to hone the flats on the chisel. Otherwise you may hone down past your hollow-grind.

4

Rock the bevel up and down on the plate until you feel it "click" into place, self-jigging on the two flats. While maintaining this position, rub the chisel forward and back. Check periodically for the burr to form. It only takes 20-30 seconds.

5

Flip the tool over onto its back to start removing the burr. Run it up and down the stone while holding it down flat.

6

Reset the chisel to the jigged position on the plate, then hop it over to the dressed strop. Draw the bevel down the strop for 5-10 strokes.

7

Flip the chisel over and lay the back down flat on the strop. Draw it down the strop for 5-10 strokes. If any burr remains, alternately strop bevel and back.

Sharpening a Plane Iron

Now, let's look at the process for hollow-grinding and honing a plane iron.

1

Sharpen a plane iron the same way. It's easier to support the iron because of its wide surface.

2

Rock the iron on the plate to find the self-jigging position, then rub forward and back until the burr forms.

3

Hone the back.

4

Find the self-jigging position on the plate, then jump it over to the strop and polish the bevel.

5

Strop the back.

SAW SHARPENING

Saw sharpening seems like an impossibly tedious task because saws have over a hundred teeth. It can be a bit of an eye test, but it's not difficult. It's just very repetitive.

The main sharpening tools are triangular files, a mill bastard file and a saw set. You can do all the angles by eye, or you can use a protractor to make a simple fleam angle guide. There are also commercial jigs.

The other specialty tool is a saw vise. This holds the saw steady while you're filing the teeth, minimizing vibration. Vibration reduces the efficiency of your filing, and makes a horrible screeching sound.

You mount the saw in the vise with the teeth just protruding above its top edge. For saws that are longer than the vise, you work the section that's in the vise, then move the saw in the vise to the next section. You can also make clamping strips for an improvised saw vise.

When filing with the triangular file, there are two angles you care about: rake and fleam.

Rake is how the teeth are pitched back at the leading edge. Ripsaws have almost vertical rake, crosscut saws are raked back as far as 60°.

Fleam is how far the teeth are filed off of 90° across the saw. Ripsaws have zero fleam, filed straight across at 90°, so they're the easiest to do. Crosscut saws have up to 25° of fleam, alternating on each side of each tooth.

Some people use different rake angles and different fleam angles depending on the type of wood they're sawing and its moisture level. There are also hybrid sharpening angles that combine rip and crosscut angles. I keep it simple and use one set of rake and fleam angles for all my ripsaws and another set for all my crosscut saws.

In addition to these filing angles, the teeth are alternately bent outward to each side just a bit. This is called set. The purpose is to widen the saw kerf slightly to prevent binding against the saw plate and allow clearing of sawdust. If a saw binds in a cut, it may not have enough set. If the cut is very ragged or the saw is hard to push, it may have too much set. If the saw tends to pull to one side, it may be set more to that side than the other.

Rake: angle of each tooth leading edge leaning back
Fleam: angle of each tooth filed off 90°
Set: alternating bend of each tooth outward

Some people like to file the teeth in a single heavy stroke. I use four light strokes, so that if one goes wrong, I can correct it on the next stroke.

Don't worry if all your strokes and teeth aren't perfectly uniform, or even if you miss a tooth or double-file one. Every saw has 100-150 teeth that all work as a team. The other teeth will make up for deficiencies in one or two. Saw sharpening is much more forgiving than edge-tool sharpening.

Sharpening a saw takes about 10 minutes. Setting the teeth also takes about 10 minutes, but it only needs to be done every five or six sharpenings.

Saws to be sharpened: full size rip and crosscut handsaws, and crosscut carcase and rip tenon joinery backsaws.

Sharpening tools: pencil, wood block for fleam angle guide, marker to highlight teeth, protractor, saw set and triangular files.

Saw vises: left, two styles of antique cast iron vises on mounting blocks; right, shop-made wooden clamshell vise with leather hinges.

Clamping strips: These allow you to clamp the saw plate in a regular vise as a quick improvised saw vise. Simply cut a strip of wood and rip a slot down its length.

To use the first vise, clamp its mounting block in the bench vise. Set the saw in place and secure the vise with the locking lever.

To use the second vise, clamp its mounting block in the bench vise. Set the saw in place and secure the vise with the thumbscrew.

To use the wooden vise, set it in the bench vise resting on its side strips, set the saw in place, and tighten the bench vise.

To use the clamping strip, slide the slot over one end of the saw and clamp in the bench vise. To work on the other end of the saw, mount the strip on that end.

General Sharpening Details for Both Rip & Crosscut Saws

While there are differences between ripsaws and crosscut saws, there are some general basics that apply to sharpening any type of saw. Let's begin by examining those before digging into specifics for different types of saws.

Color the tooth edges with a marker so you can tell which ones you've filed. Machinist's dye is also good for this.

If the teeth are uneven, joint them to the same height by running a mill bastard file flat down the length of the saw for several strokes. You only need to do this occasionally, or when you restore an old saw.

This produces shiny flats on the tips of the high teeth, leaving the shorter teeth untouched. You can joint it all at once until all the teeth have flats, or joint it a bit over several sharpenings until they're all uniform height. The sharpening process eliminates the flats and restores the points at a consistent level.

To sharpen, you drop the triangular file into each gullet and file sideways across the saw. The file is always filing the leading edge of the tooth behind it, and the trailing edge of the tooth ahead of it. It's also filing down the gullet. So you're filing three surfaces at once.

To select the appropriate size of file, check that the teeth come up about a third to halfway up the face of the file. Especially on small joinery saws, don't use an oversize file, because it will make the gullets too large.

6

The set of the teeth bends every other tooth to the opposite side, like interlacing your fingers. You only need to set a saw every five or six sharpenings, when you've filed the teeth down past the previous bend.

7

Set the teeth with a saw set. There are different designs, but most look like some type of pliers or hole punch, with adjustment for the amount of set.

8

The set has a pin that comes out and bends the tooth against the anvil when you squeeze the handle. The knobs adjust the anvil position for amount of set. Ignore any numbers or graduations. They are rough guides, not calibrated to tooth size.

9

Pick a starting tooth that needs to be set away from you. Hang the set over that tooth and squeeze the handle. Watch how far the tooth bends. The appropriate amount of set is only about a third of the sawplate thickness. Skip a tooth, then set the next tooth. Repeat for the length of the saw. Then turn the saw around in the vise and repeat for all the teeth you skipped, bending them to the other side.

After sharpening, the teeth will have small burrs on the edges. These wear off quickly in use, but you can stone the saw to remove them for a smoother cut immediately. Run a coarse sharpening stone down each side of the teeth two or three times.

10

Comparing Rip Versus Crosscut

Now let's compare the differences between ripsaws and crosscut saws.

Rip fleam: The teeth are filed straight across the saw at 90°. You file all the teeth exactly the same.

Crosscut fleam: The teeth are filed at up to 25° off 90°. You file the leading and trailing edges at opposing fleam angles.

Rip rake: The leading edges of the teeth are almost vertical. That means the top face of the file is angled down, and the back face is almost vertical.

Crosscut rake: The leading edges of the teeth are 60° back, equal to the trailing edge. That means the top face of the file is flat, and the back face is angled.

Rip set: The tips of the teeth alternate to the sides. The teeth are bent alternately toward or away from the camera in this photo.

Crosscut set: Because the fleam produces alternating points on the outside edge of the teeth, bending them outward for set creates a trough that will hold a needle or small nail.

Sharpening a Ripsaw

Now that we've examined the differences between rake and fleam of the different types of saws, let's dive into sharpening a ripsaw.

With the saw mounted in the vise, drop the file in the first gullet, oriented straight across for zero fleam, and rotate it to the desired rake angle, close to vertical. Take four light strokes. Lift the file into the next gullet and repeat. Continue in this way for every gullet down the clamped portion of the saw.

Reset the saw in the vise to continue with the next portion. Look at which teeth still have marker on them to pick up where you left off. Keep the file in a consistent orientation as you work your way along. Repeat until you reach the end of the saw. If the saw doesn't need to be set, stone it and it's ready.

If the saw needs to be set, set the teeth. Pick a starting tooth, place the set over it and squeeze the handle. Skip a tooth, set the next one. Skip, set and repeat all the way down one side, then turn the saw around and do the other. Then stone it.

Sharpening a Crosscut Saw

Crosscut saws are more complicated because of the alternating fleam. The process is as follows.

File every other gullet to one side.

Next file the skipped gullets to the other side. That forms alternating facets on the teeth.

3

You can make a simple fleam guide from a block of scrap. Using a protractor, mark a line across the block at the desired fleam angle. I use 15° off of 90°.

4

Align this line with the saw teeth. Run the block back and forth over them to cut a kerf about ¼" deep on the bottom side.

5

Flip the block over and align the kerf with the saw teeth. Run the block back and forth to cut a matching kerf on the other side.

6

Set the guide near the starting end of the saw. To find the starting gullet, look at the facets on the teeth, and find one that matches the angle the block makes across the saw. Set the file in the gullet and roll it to the desired rake angle, so that the top face of the file is horizontal. As you move the file parallel to the edge of the block at the fleam angle, you should feel it drop slightly into place to confirm you have the proper gullet.

7

Take four light strokes. Lift the end of the file, skip over a gullet, drop it into the next one, and repeat. Skip, file, skip, file. Continue in this way down the clamped portion of the saw. Move the guide ahead of the filing, and keep the file parallel to it to maintain the fleam angle.

8

Reset the guide by flipping it over to the other angle, and file all the gullets you skipped. Then reposition the saw in the vise for the next portion and repeat the process until you reach the end of the saw. If the saw doesn't need to be set, stone it and it's ready.

9

10

If the saw needs to be set, set the teeth. The proper orientation is to pick a tooth with facets that face you (as shown here) and bend it away from you.

Pick a starting tooth, place the set over it and squeeze the handle. Skip a tooth, set the next one. Skip, set, skip, set down one side, then turn the saw around and do the other. Then stone it.

Sharpening Fine Joinery Saws

Sharpening joinery saws is exactly the same. They're just more of an eye test due to the small teeth.

Dovetail saws may be 15 ppi or smaller. Use a correspondingly smaller file. For a joinery ripsaw, file at nearly vertical rake and straight across for zero fleam. If the saw doesn't need to be set, stone it and it's ready.

If the saw needs to be set, set it the same way, but now the amount of bend is tiny. Stone the saw and it's ready.

For a joinery crosscut saw, file at 60° rake, so that the top face of the file is horizontal and angled at the fleam angle. Skip every other gullet, then come back at the opposite fleam angle and file the skipped gullets. Set and stone as necessary.

CARD SCRAPER SHARPENING

The card scraper is one of the most mysterious hand tools, because there's so little to it. But it's almost magical. It's a flat, thin, flexible piece of metal that can replace a pile of sandpaper. It's great for removing machine marks, tool marks and chatter marks, and for finishing up any kind of surface to a very fine degree.

One of its magical properties is that it works in both directions, both with the grain and against it. That makes it an excellent tool for dealing with problem grain and localized surface cleanup.

There are many variations of the procedure for sharpening a card scraper, but they all follow a similar pattern. The steps are burnishing to unroll the old hook, jointing, honing and burnishing to roll the new hook.

The initial burnishing step unrolls the old hook so that your fingernails no longer catch on it. Some people don't bother with this step.

Jointing flattens the edge and files off the hook, like jointing the edge of a board.

Honing polishes out the file marks from jointing and sharpens the long corner of the edge.

The final burnishing step rolls the sharpened edge to form the new hook.

Rolling the hook is where people run into problems. The other steps are clear-cut, but burnishing has a lot of variability in how much pressure to use, how many strokes to take and what angle to use. That's what makes it frustrating for beginners, because any of these can ruin an otherwise good sharpening. The biggest problem is in over-rolling the hook past the point of effectiveness.

Because the scraper has two long sides and each side has two faces, you can actually put four hooked edges on it. The hooks are fairly delicate, so the sharp edges wear away in use. As one hook starts to lose effectiveness, just flip the scraper around to another one.

Here I'll show two sharpening methods, a traditional method and a simplified method. The simplified method distills the traditional method. I've gone through half a dozen scraper sharpening methods over the years, and this simplified method is now my preferred method due to its speed, simplicity and effectiveness.

The secret of the scraper's action is in the little hook that's formed on the edge. When you run your fingers down the face of the scraper over the edge, your fingernails catch on it. Don't run your finger along the edge, that's where it's sharp.

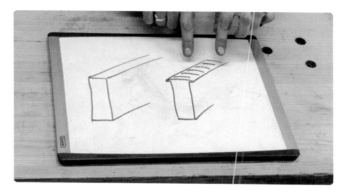

This diagram illustrates the scraper before and after rolling the hooks on one long edge. Left, the jointing and honing steps produce the sharp corners along the long, flat edge at top. Right, the burnishing process mushrooms the metal outward, pushing those sharpened corners out to form the hooks on each side. Over-rolling the edge bends the hooks around too far so that they no longer catch in the wood.

Using the Scraper

Before we examine the sharpening of this tool, let's take a quick look at how the scraper is used.

1

Flex the scraper to form a cambered cutting edge. It's made of flexible spring steel, similar to the steel in saws. You can make custom scrapers out of pieces of old saw plates.

2

Tip the flexed scraper up and down on the wood until you feel the hook catch.

3

Push forward while maintaining this angle. Extend your arms as you lean your body forward to make it a full-body motion.

4

A sharp scraper should produce wispy rolled up curls, though different woods will respond it to it differently. If you're just getting dust, that means the scraper needs sharpening, or it's not sharpened properly.

A Traditional Sharpening Method

As mentioned, I'll show you a couple of methods for sharpening the scraper. Let's start with a traditional method – you can later decide if you prefer it or the simplified approach at the end of this section.

1

The sharpening setup consists of a burnisher, a mill bastard file, a slotted wooden holder that acts as a clamping aid and sharpening stones. These are oilstones, but other types work as well.

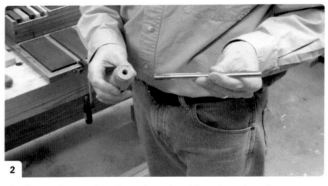

2

This burnisher is a hardened steel rod fitted in a handle.

3

Use the logo on the scraper to identify front and back, top and bottom. Otherwise it's easy to lose track as you're sharpening and flipping the scraper around. The four hook edges will be top front, top back, bottom front and bottom back.

4

For a scraper without a clear and unambiguous logo, scribe a cabinetmaker's triangle on it with a sharp object. This marks the front face, with the tip of the triangle indicating the top.

5

To flatten out the old burr, lay the scraper flat on the bench near the edge. Run the burnisher flat across the edge back and forth off the ends. That will make a clicking sound like an old-fashioned ticketing machine, so this is called ticketing. Some people refer to the burnisher as a ticketer. Repeat on all four hook edges.

6

To joint the scraper, slide the holder over the scraper and clamp it in the bench vise. Set the file down across the scraper edge, perpendicular to the faces. Align the teeth on the top side of the file with the scraper edge. That means the teeth on the underside will be oriented diagonally across the edge. Pressing down with moderate pressure, run the file along the edge. This is called draw filing. You'll feel the teeth bite into the scraper. Make several passes until the edge is straight and clean. If the edge is very uneven, you can orient the file longways, like a handplane down the edge of a board. It will take the high spots down and flatten the edge. Flip the scraper in the vise and repeat on the other edge.

7

To hone the filed edge, remove the scraper from the holder and stand it on edge on the coarse sharpening stone with some oil. Run it back and forth, holding it carefully to maintain it perfectly upright at 90° and avoid cutting your hand on the sharp corners. Repeat on the other edge.

8

Lay the scraper flat on the edge of the stone and run it up and down the stone. This hones the face where it meets the honed edge. Flip it over and repeat on the other face. Then repeat this on the other edge. This is where it's easy to lose track of which faces you've done, so do it in order of top front, top back, bottom front and bottom back.

Repeat these honing steps on the remaining stones. I use an auxiliary holder stacked over the rightmost stone in my sharpening station so I can hone the scraper faces on each one, then finish on that stone.

9

10

To start rolling the edges, put the scraper back in the holder, with the T on the holder oriented to match the top front of the scraper, and clamp it in the vise. This is where you really need to pay attention so you don't roll the same edge twice. Lay the burnisher flat across the edge; with medium pressure, run the burnisher down the edge to start mushrooming the hook edges out. Take several passes back and forth. The number of strokes depends on how much pressure you use. This is where the variability in the process starts to come in. But it takes less than you might think. It's tempting to push down hard, but that's not necessary.

11

12

To complete rolling the edge, pitch the burnisher down about 10° and take several strokes at this angle. This rolls the mushroomed edge over to its final position. Your fingernails should catch on this hook. Turn the scraper and holder around in the vise and repeat on the back side. Then flip the scraper to the bottom and do the bottom front and back edges.

The rolling step is highly variable. You can control some of that variability by laying the scraper down flat on the bench and running the tip of the burnisher down the underside of the hook. This slightly unrolls it. By doing this with the burnisher at a consistent angle, you can get a more consistent hook on all four edges. There are also special burnishers that have a ground tip to do this. But the curved tip, held at an angle, is effective. The scraper is now ready to use.

A useful exercise is to lay the scraper down, lightly ticket the edges to unroll them, and test it. Then lightly reroll the edges. You can adjust the hooks this way to fine tune and even restore them for use once or twice. Eventually they'll wear or weaken to the point that you need to do a full resharpening.

13

A Simplified Method

This method omits ticketing and simplifies usage of the stones. Leaving the scraper in the vise speeds up some of the steps.

This method takes less than two minutes to sharpen all four hooks, versus about five minutes for the other method.

The setup is similar. The burnisher doesn't have a handle, and the stone is a piece of fine India stone. The reason for removing the burnisher handle is to keep you from applying too much leverage and over-rolling the burr. This particular stone is a combination coarse/fine, but you don't need the coarse side.

Slide the scraper into the holder and mount it in the vise. Run the file across the scraper, holding it level.

If the scraper edge isn't perfectly straight, you can joint it flat by holding the file lengthwise and running it down the edge.

Spread a drop of oil on the fine India stone. Lay it level on the scraper edge and run it back and forth 5-10 strokes to polish out the file marks.

Repeat on the front face of the scraper.

Repeat on the back face.

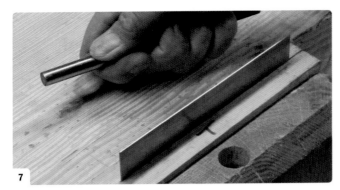

7

Burnisher handling is critical. To further limit how much force you apply, choke up on it until only an inch or so is exposed.

8

Set the burnisher flat across the scraper edge and take two light strokes, one forward, one back, to lightly mushroom the edge. Just two quick swipes is all it takes. Use your other hand only as a guide, not to apply more force. You can also do this one handed.

Tip the burnisher down 5-10° and take two light strokes forward and back to roll the edge. Be careful not to use too much force. Just two quick swipes is all it takes. I've seen it described as the amount of force you would use when slicing a steak with a sharp knife. Tip the burnisher the other way and repeat on the top back edge. Then flip the scraper and holder over in the vise and repeat the entire process on the bottom front and back edges.

9

CHAPTER 3
STOCK PREPARATION

GAUGES, SQUARES & MARKING KNIVES

Marking tools are essential to fine joinery. Bad marking will ruin good parts. The primary marking tools are marking gauges, squares and marking knives.

Even tools as simple as these require practice. Marking skills are not something you want to be developing in the middle of a project.

Marking Gauges

Many different types of marking gauges exist. Despite difference in construction they all do the same thing. At the end of the day a marking gauge is simply an adjustable device with a steel pin or knife that marks a layout line parallel to a wood edge. In the following photos we'll examine a few different types of gauges and how they are used.

Three types of marking gauges. They can be surprisingly awkward to handle at first. Set a gauge by moving the sliding fence to a specific distance from its pin or cutter in one of two ways. Hold a ruler up to the pin or knife and set the fence to a measurement, or hold the gauge up to a workpiece or a mark on the workpiece and set it to that.

This commercial dual-pin marking gauge has a single pin on one side, and two pins on the other side. These can be set to a specific width for marking mortises and tenons. The knob on the fence locks it in place on the beam. To set this type of fence to a precise measurement, loosen the knob so you can slide it to rough position, snug it up a bit, then tap one end of the beam or the other on the bench to micro-adjust the position. Then fully tighten the knob. This gauge has a screw at the far end to set the width of the dual pins. Simpler gauges just use a sliding bar.

Here's a shop-made cutting gauge made by a friend of mine. The cutting knife marks more cleanly than pins do, which is why I like this style. Set the fence on this one like the pin gauge. The knob on the end secures the knife. Normally, you mount the knife with the bevel facing the fence. That makes it track better, pulling the fence tight up to the wood. Occasionally you may need to reverse the knife to keep the bevel on the waste side of the line. That leaves a crisp cut wall on the good side.

This commercial cutting wheel marking gauge has a beveled wheel. To set the fence on this one, loosen both locking screws and slide the fence to rough position. Fully tighten the far knob, then micro-adjust the position by turning the knurled barrel. Fully tighten the second knob. This can be done one-handed while holding it to a ruler or a mark.

You can find the center of a board thickness quickly with a marking gauge, no measuring required. Set the gauge approximately to the center. Hold the fence of the gauge tight to one side of the board and roll the pin over to just dimple the wood. Then hold the fence against the opposite side and dimple the wood from that side. This will leave two small pin pricks in the wood, equidistant from the center; the first one is just visible here next to the pin. Set the gauge to the midpoint from these marks.

Running the gauge along the board is where people tend to have problems. Set the fence tight up against the side of the board and pay attention to which way the grain is moving in from the edge. Pin gauges tend to track in the grain. Pull or push the gauge so that it follows the grain in from the edge. This pulls the fence in tight against the edge. If you go the other direction, the grain may pull it off course, out toward the edge. Tip the gauge so that the pin is trailing as you move it. Don't stand it up straight; that causes it to catch and jump. Make several light passes rather than trying to make one heavy, deep pass.

Mark end grain the same way, but from both sides into the center to avoid breakout at the end. From the far corner, tip the gauge and pull it toward you as you hold the fence tight against the workpiece. On the near corner, tip the gauge the other way and push it away from you, keeping the fence on the same side of the workpiece. It's helpful to clamp the workpiece in the vise so you can free up both hands to guide the gauge. Use several light passes each way to deepen the line.

As you get used to handling the gauge, you can hold the workpiece with one hand and run the gauge with the other, pulling or pushing as necessary as you press the fence tight up against the board. This is another way to grip the gauge.

Hold the workpiece down on the bench to steady it.

Mark on the face the same way, pulling or pushing depending on the grain as you hold the fence tight against the edge. This workpiece has reversing grain, so the near part must be marked by pulling, and the far part by pushing.

Mark across the grain while holding the workpiece overhanging on the bench. The pin will have more tendency to jump, so use light passes. It can also leave a torn line.

To reduce the dragging and tearing, sharpen the sides of the pin to a flat point using a diamond stick or sandpaper wrapped around a piece of scrap. That shapes it more like a knife cutter. Sharpen a little more heavily on the side facing the fence to put a bevel on it that will help it pull tight to the fence as it tracks.

Use a cutting gauge the same as a pin gauge, tipping it to trail the knife point while holding the fence tight up against the board, making several light passes. Marking an edge along the grain.

Marking end grain, from both ends into the middle.

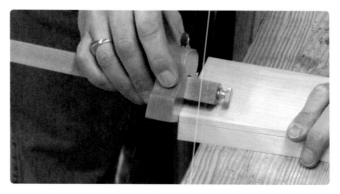

Marking across the grain. Cutting gauges work especially well on cross grain, because they slice cleanly across the fibers.

Comparing cross-grain markings from a cutting gauge (left) and a pin gauge (right). The cutting gauge line is clean and crisp. The pin gauge line has torn edges, though sharpening the pin improves that.

The cutting gauge line provides a good registration to set a chisel edge into.

Use a wheel cutting gauge like the other two, pushing or pulling with the fence tight up against the board. However, the round wheel means you don't have to tip the gauge. You can also roll it along rather than dragging it. This is useful for small marks or awkward spots because you have very precise control of how far you roll it.

Marking end grain, from both ends into the middle.

Marking cross grain. Like the knife, the wheel leaves a very clean line.

The cutters on all three of the gauges are beveled, so that they pull the fence in tight against the edge.

Squares

As with marking gauges, there are several different types of squares that for the most part perform the same main functions: measuring, marking, determining angles and checking the correctness of right angles.

Three types of squares: a small engineer's square, a combination square and a shop-made wooden square.

A

B

C

Check your squares periodically. **(A)** Butt the stock tight up against a jointed edge and draw a line across. **(B)** Flip the square over, butt it up tight against the edge, and draw a second line next to the first. **(C)** Check the lines. If they're parallel, the square is accurate. If they diverge or cross, the square is out-of-square. This may be the result of dropping the square on a hard floor.

You may be able to correct a combination square by careful filing in the slots. Engineer's squares are more difficult to correct, so may need to be discarded. When you make a wooden square, you true it up as the last step by planing the edge of the blade. It's easy to repeat this if you need to correct the square later.

To use a square, butt the stock up against the workpiece. Use your thumb to hold it tight there and your fingers to hold the blade down flat. Keep your fingers back from the edge so they don't get in the way of your pencil or marking knife.

A reverse grip from the other edge, using your fingers to pull the stock against it.

When checking an edge for square, push the stock of the square up flat against the face. Make sure it's not pitched outward.

Marking Knives

Utility knives, craft knives, penknives and chip-carving knives can all be used for marking, as well as knives made specifically for marking. The key is that it comes to a sharp point. Some people also like to have separate beveled knives, one with a left bevel and one with a right bevel, for marking on different sides of a square.

The main reason for using a knife line instead of a pencil line is obvious when you compare the two. The knife line is much finer and more precise. But there are functional reasons as well. You can set the point of the knife in the line, bring the square up to it, and make repeated passes to deepen it. You can set the edge of a chisel in it for precise registration. The marking knife is also the first cutting tool on the wood when doing fine joinery, cutting the surface layers of wood cleanly.

You can run the knife down the waste side of the line to form a small trough to set your saw into. This is called a "knifewall."

This gives you very precise placement of the saw cut. This is the process for producing first-class cuts, where accuracy and appearance count, because the cut is precisely positioned and has a clean edge. The knifewall also provides a precise registration surface for a chisel.

1

The procedure for marking a line all the way around a piece accurately depends on having one edge marked as the reference edge, and one face marked as the reference face. Following the procedure rigorously ensures the lines will meet at the last corner, even if the piece is not perfectly squared up. This piece has a "V" on the edge and a cursive "F" on the face, marking the reference edge and reference face. The point of the "V" meets the tail of the "F". There is already a knife line across the reference face.

2

The rule is to always butt the square up against a reference surface. To mark this edge, butt the square up against the reference face. Always set the knife at the marking position and slide the square over to meet it. Then knife along the square, using several light passes to get the desired depth.

3

To mark this face, butt the square against the reference edge. Set the knife in the end of the previous line for position, bring the square over to it, and knife the line.

4

To mark this last edge, butt the square against the reference face. That means you have to reverse the square. Set the knife in the end of the previous line, bring the square over and knife the line.

5

The lines have met up at that last corner.

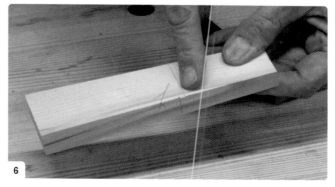

6

To prove to yourself that this works, take a workpiece that is tapered in width and thickness and mark a line all around, but keep the square in the same orientation all around. The last corner will be off like this, because you've marked a spiral around the piece. Then mark a line all around again, but use the reference marks as described above. The last corner will meet up.

ROUGH STOCK PREPARATION

The simplest classifications of work are "rough" and "fine." Rough work is all about speed and efficiency. Fine work is about appearance and accuracy. Rough work is about getting the bulk of the work done, using the tool that takes the biggest bite. Fine work is about the last little bit, those last little fine details.

Another way to look at it is as coarse, medium and fine. Using this approach, coarse is rough work (the bulk of the job), medium takes it down to the next level, and fine is your last very fine details.

The fine work removes very small amounts of wood. It is usually more time consuming than the rough work despite the difference in the amount of wood removed.

For crosscuts, there are three classes of cut: third-class, second-class and first-class. Third-class cuts are rough cuts, where appearance and accuracy are not an issue. Second-class cuts are finer cuts, where accuracy is an issue. First-class cuts are the very finest cuts, where both appearance and accuracy matter.

Rough stock preparation is the process of breaking down full-size lumber to roughly dimensioned parts, using third-class cuts. You're working to about the nearest ⅛" to 1" accuracy. The larger the margin you leave, the more you can tolerate errors, but the more material you leave for cleanup at the fine stage.

Don't cut exactly to final dimension. Either layout rough cut lines a little outside the finished dimensions and cut on those, or do the cutting on the waste side of the final lines, leaving some margin.

The three cut orientations are crosscutting, ripping and resawing. Crosscutting is across the grain – cutting to length. Ripping is with the grain – cutting to width. Resawing is also with the grain, but for the full width of the board – cutting to thickness. Ripping and resawing may seem like a lot of work, but even in harder woods, it's not that difficult one piece at a time. Take breaks and pace yourself.

Don't worry about how ugly the cuts turn out, as long as you don't go past your line. No matter how ragged, bumpy or out-of-square they are, you'll clean them up in seconds with handplanes later on. That's the teamwork of handsaws and handplanes. Work to whatever tolerance you're comfortable with at your current skill level. If you think you can cut right to that line, go ahead and do it. But if you need space, give yourself whatever margin allows you to complete the cut without going past your line.

Sharp tools are critical to speed and efficiency here. If your saws aren't sharp, sharpen them before you begin. If a saw starts to dull in use, stop to sharpen it. The difference between how dull and sharp saws work is amazing.

A sawbench, similar to a sawhorse, but wide enough to set the board on top. It has a ripping notch at one end. There are a variety of different designs. Size the sawbench for you to be able to place one knee on the work to hold it down. Make two for working on longer boards, to support the other end and catch offcuts.

Use sharp rip and crosscut saws. Lubricate them by scribbling lightly on both sides with with wax. Use a block of beeswax or paraffin, a candle or a smear of furniture pastewax on a cloth. Lubrication reduces the friction in the cut, making for smoother cutting. You can also use an oil wick, a tightly rolled piece of cloth sticking out of a small can. Moisten the end with mineral or light machine oil. Run the wick over the saws, or set it in a holder on the bench and run the saws over it.

Crosscutting

Let's start with crosscutting a board to length – again, this means that you'll be cutting across the grain.

1

Set the board on the sawbench with the cut line just overhanging the end of the bench. Place your off-hand knee and leg on the board to hold it down. You'll be sawing across the board in front of your body, with your arm free to drive the saw. To start the cut, pinch the corner of the board at the end of the cut line and rest the saw on the corner, using your fingers as a guide, about a third of the way down the length of the saw. Start with little nibbling cuts back and forth to get the kerf started.

2

Use the trigger-finger grip. Once the kerf is started, take steady, full-length strokes, with the saw angled down at about 45°. This is all about smoothness and control, it's not about power. Let gravity and the sharp teeth do their job.

3

At the end of the cut, raise the saw angle up and take smaller strokes to finish cleanly. Support the offcut so it doesn't fall and pull off a long splinter.

4

Body mechanics and alignment are important to ensure a smooth cut. Line up shoulder, elbow and wrist with the tip of the saw in the same plane, so that you have a smooth piston action extending and reversing. If you're out of alignment, it will pull or push the saw off course or twist it to the side.

Ripping
Now let's rip a board to width – cutting with the grain.

1

2

Ripping a piece down its entire length is where the magic of spring steel comes in. When you drive a car down the street, you don't hold the steering wheel dead in your hands and just go straight, you're constantly adjusting to correct as the wheels respond to the road, even on a straight road. A saw is just the same. As you saw down the rip, you can actually pull the saw from one side to the other to correct and steer it.

Set the board on the sawbench with the cut line over the ripping notch on the end of the bench. This time, place your on-hand knee and leg on the board to clamp it down. You'll be sawing down the board in front of your body again, pushing the board further along the bench every few strokes. To start the cut, pinch the end of the board at the end of the cut line and rest the saw on the corner, using your fingers as a guide, about a third of the way down the length of the saw. Draw back for a couple of strokes to get the rip teeth started, then use little nibbling cuts back and forth until you can switch to steady, full-length strokes at about 45°, using the trigger-finger grip. Once the cut reaches the halfway point, turn the board around and complete the cut from the other end.

3

4

If the saw starts to track away from the cut line, lower the angle and pull the saw sideways back toward the line. The steering is actually very subtle, just small bends. This photo exaggerates the bend for illustration. Take a few strokes this way until it's back on track, then straighten it out and raise it back up to 45°. If you maintain this steering continually, you'll only need to make small corrections. With practice, you'll be able to saw right on a pencil line for the entire length of a board.

If you don't have a sawbench, or you find leaning over to cut bothers your back, secure the piece overhanging the end of the workbench and cut it there. This is a good use for holdfasts. Hit them on top with a mallet to set them, hit them on the back of the neck to release them. Stand further back from the bench and saw at a lower angle if you find it awkward raising the saw as you cut.

5

6

To rip at the bench, secure the piece overhanging the front edge of the workbench and cut it there. Lower the angle of the saw as necessary to steer it. This setup allows you to cut all the way from one end to the other without moving the piece.

An alternate grip for efficient two-handed sawing: Wrap your thumbs around the horns of the handles and push the saw up and down at high angle.

7

For a piece that's too short to rip on the sawbench, rip it on top of the workbench, or secure it in the vise and rip down halfway, then turn the piece over and rip the other half. Kneel on one knee so you can saw at about 45°, or saw from standing position if kneeling is uncomfortable, dropping the saw to as low an angle as you can.

Resawing

Now let's cut a board for thickness. You'll be cutting with the grain here.

Resawing is the heaviest kind of cut. Do all other cuts first to get the piece down to its smallest size and minimize the amount of resawing. Use this for making bookmatched parts, or to thin down stock without wasting it all by planing. Secure the piece in the vise with a corner up high. Start the cut across the corner. This cut must be straight both down the width of the piece and across the end grain.

You can continue two ways. First, once the cut is halfway across the end grain, flip the piece in the vise and start on the matching corner. Second, keep sawing until you have a full-width diagonal across the piece. Either way, keep flipping the piece over and cutting across the point of the interior remaining wood. The established kerf will help guide the saw. Repeated flipping also helps you keep track of the cut and correct it if it starts going off on the underside. You can lower the saw and extend the cut further down the length. Once you get halfway down the length of the piece, repeat the process on the other end until it meets up with the first end.

The completed cut will leave rough faces that will need to be planed flat. Depending on how well your cut turned out, resawing and planing can consume anywhere from 1/16" to 1/4" of material, so plan for this loss when you select the thickness, based on your current skill level.

ROUGH-SAWING EXERCISE

This exercise helps you develop control of the saws, working out any problems on cheap softwood practice lumber before you try it on good lumber. Then practice on hardwood.

If a cut doesn't turn out as well as you expected, take a moment to figure out what went wrong and try to correct that on the next cut. That's the reason for doing multiple identical cuts.

Save all the pieces for later practice exercises.

1

Layout a practice board with three repeated crosscuts, two long rips and three smaller crosscuts and rips. You'll cut on these lines. Make sure your saws are sharp and lubricated with wax or an oil wick.

2

Do the end crosscuts. Remember to use the trigger finger grip.

3

Do the long rip cuts.

4

Crosscut the first short length to be ripped. Cut off the remaining two lengths as one piece, so that you leave one last crosscut in them.

5

Rip these pieces in half.

6

Crosscut the remaining pieces in a pair of bench hooks. Having two hooks allows you to spread them apart as far as necessary to support the piece.

7 Hook the front of the hooks on the front of the bench and push the piece tight up against the rear of the hooks with the cut line overhanging. Don't cut between the hooks.

8 Crosscut flat across.

9 Cut the second piece with a joinery crosscut backsaw that is sharp and lubricated.

10 Use some of the small resulting rectangles for resawing practice.

HANDPLANE FIST FIGHTS & FUNDAMENTALS

There are three main arguments about handplanes: bevel orientation, number of planes to use and body type.

Bevel orientation refers to the way the iron sits in the plane. Shown here are a low angle bevel-up bench plane (front) and a bevel-down bench plane (back).

In the bevel-up plane, the iron sits with the bevel facing up **(A)**. In the bevel-down plane, the iron sits in the plane with the bevel facing down **(B)**. Except for early planes, most bevel-down planes have a chipbreaker mounted on the back of the iron, also known as a double iron. Sometimes people confuse the chipbreaker for the cutting bevel. The function of the chipbreaker is to curl the chip upward as the cutting edge lifts it off the wood.

For bench planes, while bevel-down planes are more common, there are plenty of people who swear by their bevel-up planes, in various sizes. Block planes are bevel-up.

Number of planes refers to having a dedicated plane for each of the three functions of roughing, flattening and smoothing (versus using a single, versatile plane for all functions, with different irons and setups). A three-plane setup like this consists of smoother, jack and jointer planes (front to back); each one is dedicated to a specific purpose. Jack planes tend to be the ones used for multiple purposes, especially with bevel-up planes.

Body type refers to wooden or metal planes, and overall design. Left to right are three wooden styles: an antique all-wooden plane, a transitional metal and wooden plane, a modern wooden plane and two metal bodied planes. Another style of metal bodied plane is an infill plane, not shown. All of these types work, as evidenced by the work people have done with them. Each one has its own balance and feel. Switching between planes is a little like switching between different types of vehicles when you're driving. You need to relearn the skills a bit as you go from one to another. Whichever style you use, make sure it holds its iron well. A plane that slips and won't hold its adjustment is extremely frustrating to use.

There's nothing wrong with mixing styles. Use whichever plane works well for you for a particular function. This is a perfectly good three-plane setup, all different.

A comparison of edge shavings taken off the same board by three different tools: a wooden jack plane, a #7 jointer and a #4 smoother. This is a perfect example of coarse, medium and fine, showing what it means to use the tool that takes the biggest bite. The jack shaving is the thickness of cardboard, the jointer shaving is the thickness of printer paper, and the smoother shaving is the thickness of tissue paper. With the irons at these current depths, the jack shaving that this plane produces is three-four times the thickness of the jointer shaving, which is in turn about 10 times the thickness of the smoother shaving that this plane produces. One stroke of the jack is equal to three or four of the jointer, and it's equal to 20 or 30 of the smoother. That's why it's important to use the plane appropriate to the job you're doing. That's what makes the work efficient.

(A) With a dial caliper, the heavy jack shaving measures at just over $3/100$". **(B)** The medium jointer shaving comes in at just under $1/100$". **(C)** The thin smoother shaving doesn't even register.

FINE STOCK PREPARATION

Fine stock preparation is dimensioning lumber precisely along faces, edges and ends with handplanes. The sequence of operations is known by the acronym FEW-TEL. It consists of planing the first Face, the first Edge, the second edge, which produces the final Width, the second face, which produces the final Thickness, the first End, and the second end, which produces the Length.

Just as rough sawing broke the lumber down in three dimensions, the FEWTEL sequence takes it down to final size in three dimensions, in width, thickness and length. This is where precision counts, down to a fraction of a degree and a thousandth of an inch. One of the amazing things about working with hand tools is that with practice, they allow you to work to this level of precision.

The first face and edge become your reference surfaces. These are critical to proper dimensioning and joinery. Everything else is based on them. Once you have them flat and straight, with the edge square to the face, you make the opposite surfaces parallel to them. You take all your measurements from your reference surfaces, and you always place gauge fences and square heads against them. Consistency using reference surfaces is a major factor in how well things fit.

This is where sharp tools are absolutely critical to speed, efficiency and precision. If your tools aren't sharp, sharpen them before doing this. If a tool starts to dull in use, stop to sharpen it. Just like saws, the difference between how dull and sharp planes work is amazing.

Handplaning is not just an arm motion, it's a whole body motion. You have your whole upper body mass over your legs to bring to the work. That's a 50- to 100-pound mass, on a 4- to 6-foot lever arm. As you plane, lean into it with your whole body.

F is the first face. E is the first edge, square to the reference face. W is the second edge, parallel to the reference edge at a measured distance, establishing the width. T is the second face, parallel to the reference face at a measured distance, establishing the thickness. E is the first end, square to the reference edge and reference face. L is the second end, parallel to the first end at a measured distance, establishing the length; it is also square to the reference edge and face.

As with handsaws, use sharp handplanes and lubricate the bottom with wax or an oil wick. Use the trigger finger grip while planing.

Depending on how your bench is set up, there are several ways to hold the work for face planing. I like to use battens on my bench. One clamps in the vise and the other has dowels that fit into the dog holes.

Push the workpiece up against the battens. One batten serves as an end stop and one as a side stop. You don't need to clamp your workpiece down because the force of planing will pin it up against them. This is faster than securing the piece to the top, especially if you need to reorient it or flip it over.

Drive the planing stop up with a mallet to support the clamped batten from behind.

You can also use a planing board, which is like a large bench hook. It has a hook edge on the front, with shallow stop edges on the side and back. Push it up against a bench dog or a planing stop, or clamp the hook edge in the vise. Then plane into the stop edges the same as the battens.

The general order of operations is roughing, flattening and smoothing, using the medium size #5 jack plane (left), the long #7 jointer plane (center), and the short #4 smoothing plane (right). The edges of pieces are generally used straight off the jointer, without any additional smoothing. The smoothing plane is typically only used on the faces of boards. But it can also be the tool of choice when you need to do something using a smaller, lighter plane.

In order to do fast, heavy roughing, the #5 has a cambered iron (left). The jointer and the smoother have irons ground straight across (right). If the wood is already close to the final dimension, you can skip the roughing step.

The irons and their chipbreakers. The chipbreaker of the #5 is set far away from the edge. The chipbreaker of the #7 is close to the edge. The #4 is even closer. This means the #5 will take rough, heavy shavings; the #7 will take fine shavings; and #4 smoother will take the very finest shavings.

Preparing the First Face (F)

1

To plane the reference face (the F step), start by roughing it across the grain, called "traversing." First, run the #5 jack along the far edge with it tipped over at an angle to take off the back corner. This avoids breakout there when you traverse across the grain. Breakout like that is called "spelching."

2

Take overlapping strokes straight across the grain. The cambered iron will leave a scalloped surface. Traversing allows you to set the plane for a heavier chip than you could do along the grain. That's the secret to fast roughing of a face.

3

If you just use your arms, you'll tire quickly. Proper body mechanics are to use your whole body. Lean in as you push and extend. That gives you more power and endurance when planing.

4

If the grain is resisting you, skew the plane diagonally and push straight back. Skewing reduces the effective angle of the cut. It's often a useful tactic for dealing with problem grain.

5

6

Check the surface for twist, or wind (as in winding a clock), using winding sticks. These are just scraps of aluminum angle iron. You can also make traditional winding sticks. Either way, they need to be straight and flat. Set them across the ends of the board parallel to each other.

Sight directly across the top of the sticks. If the board is perfectly flat, the tops should be parallel. If they're not, the board has a high corner, or two high corners diagonally across from each other. The length of the sticks exaggerates the amount of wind, making it easier to see than just looking across the board itself. Move each stick closer to the opposite end repeatedly and sight across to figure out where the twist occurs. It may be twisted evenly down its length or flat in some places but twisted in others. Use a single stick as a straightedge across the board to check for cupping upward or downward. Use a stick or longer straightedge to check along the length of the board.

7

8

Plane diagonally, high corner to high corner, to remove the twist. For a single high spot, plane selectively over that. Don't take too much off at once or you'll over-correct and have to take down the opposite diagonal. Check with the winding sticks and repeat as necessary.

To set the jointer depth of cut for flattening, sight down the bed from the heel as you turn the depth adjustment knob to advance or retract the iron, and move the lateral adjustment lever to get it straight across. For your first couple of passes, use a deeper cut, which will take off the high points left by roughing.

Start with overlapping diagonal passes, straightening out to full-length overlapping passes. The shavings will be very small as the plane removes those high points, but will rapidly grow in size. Don't plane repeatedly in the same spot, move uniformly across the entire surface. Otherwise you'll make a low spot and have to bring everything else down to that.

9

10

As the plane starts to take fuller, heavier shavings, back off the depth of the iron to reduce the resistance. You can adjust the iron while holding the plane over the work with one or two flicks of your finger and thumb. If you retract the iron so far that it no longer cuts, advance it back out. It's easier to take more passes of lighter cuts than fewer passes of heavier cuts.

11 A

11 B

It's important to control the pressure down on the plane ends at the start and end of the cut. Otherwise, you may round over the ends of the piece. At the start of the cut **(A)**, place all the down force on the front of the plane, as if you weren't holding the tote with your rear hand. This keeps the back end of the plane from drooping. As the plane moves fully onto the piece, transfer the force equally to both hands. At the end of the cut **(B)**, place all the down force on the back of the plane, as if you weren't holding the knob with your front hand. This keeps the front end from drooping. You don't actually need to let go of the plane during the stroke, but this illustrates how to transfer the force between your hands (and is a useful way to practice that transfer).

12

If the grain is hard to work, skew the plane and push it straight down the length of the piece. Skewing a tool is often an effective strategy to improve the cut in a variety of operations.

13

Once again, body mechanics are extremely important. Don't just stand upright and push with your hands, lean your upper body into the cut as you extend your arms, to put the momentum of your whole body mass behind it. Your body is like an upside down pendulum, pivoting on your hips, feet and legs. For a longer piece, do this in overlapping sections, shuffling forward a step at a time.

Normally, you plane with the grain. Here I've highlighted the grain direction to show how it rises toward the far end of the board. Plane with that rising direction. As an exercise, turn the board around and plane against the grain to see what it's like. The difference is minor in some woods, but extremely pronounced in others; it also depends on the specific grain in a particular piece. It will be harder to do and leave a rougher surface, with the potential to cause tear-out (leaving a ragged surface) or chip-out (removing large chips).

Aim to finish each stroke with the iron out past the end of the piece. That adds a little follow-through so you don't end up stopping short of the end. Because the iron is actually located roughly in the middle of the plane, make sure that point goes past the end of the work with a smooth motion.

Use the plane body as a straightedge to check for uneven spots, across the piece and along its length. If you see light under it, that indicates a low spot. You can also pencil in some lines across and along the piece to form a grid, then plane it. Anywhere the pencil is left behind is a low spot. Plane the rest of the surface down flush with the low spots using overlapping passes.

Check for final flatness using winding sticks. Once you're satisfied with it, set your smoother for a light cut to do final smoothing. This should not change the flatness as long as you plane the entire surface consistently.

18

19

For final smoothing, plane the surface in overlapping passes with the #4 plane. You might want to save this step for later after assembly on surfaces that will be accessible, to clean up any marks, dents or scratches that may occur in the meantime.

Mark the reference face. The traditional mark is a lower-case cursive "f," where the tail runs off the edge that will be the reference edge.

Preparing the Reference Edge (E)

1

To plane the reference edge, the E step, mount the piece in the vise with the edge facing upward and the grain on the adjacent face rising up away from you. Set the jack plane for a relatively thick cut, especially if you need to remove a lot of material. Hook your thumb behind the knob, with your fingers wrapped under the plane so that your index finger runs along the face as a guide. Lean into the cut and extend your arms as you plane.

2

If the wood is difficult to work, skew the plane and either plane across in short diagonal nibbles, or run the skewed plane down the length of the edge. The diagonal nibbles allow you to take a very heavy cut, then you can return to straight planing.

3

Flattening an edge is known as "jointing." This is where you really need to pay careful attention to the angle of the plane, because your goal is to plane this edge perfectly square to the face. This is part of training your body to recognize what 90° is like. Rest the plane flat on the edge with your thumb hooked around the knob, your fingers wrapped under the body to act as a fence against the wood. Initially this just takes tiny shavings as it cleans up the uneven surface left by the roughing plane, but the shavings quickly get wider and heavier. Start dialed in for a heavy cut, then back it off as the shavings get consistent, finishing with a light cut to sneak up to the line precisely.

 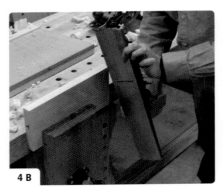 

(A) Thumb hooked behind knob, **(B)** fingers wrapped under bed, **(C)** from below showing fingers wrapped.

 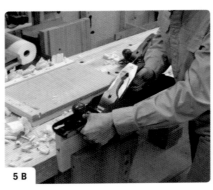 

As with face planing, you need to manage the transfer of pressure across your hands so the plane doesn't droop at the start or end of the cut. **(A)** Press down on the front of the plane to start. **(B)** Transfer to both hands evenly as the plane passes over the piece. **(C)** Then transfer primarily to the back of the plane to finish. As an exercise, try using just enough rear hand grip to hold the plane up when starting and remove your front hand when finishing.

 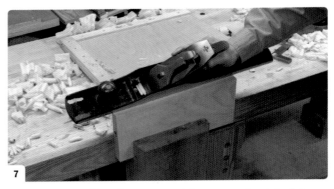

Check periodically with a square at multiple points along the edge so you can correct the edge before it gets too far out of square. Look for light coming under the square, indicating an edge that is not square.

Use the corner of the plane or a straightedge to check for flatness. Look for light coming under the edge, indicating low spots. Low spots in the center mean you need to keep planing down to bring the rest of the edge even with them. Low spots at the ends mean you've let the plane droop and rounded the board.

8

An out-of-square edge. With the square held up tight to the board, light is visible at the back edge. That means the front edge is high. To bring it down even with the back edge to restore the edge to squareness, center the plane over the high edge. There's nothing to support it on the sides, so you have to hold it balanced at 90°. Take two or three careful passes of light shavings. These will produce very narrow shavings as they begin to produce a flat across that edge. Rest the plane on that flat and take another couple shavings. Check with the square. Keep centering the plane on the flat as it grows wider while you take more shavings. It will get wide enough to support the plane and give you a good registration surface. Stop once the edge is full width and square across. It's very easy to overcorrect and go the other way, or produce a high ridge in the center. Either way, center the plane on the high spot and take careful, light shavings until you get a square edge.

9

Mark the reference edge. The traditional mark is a "V," where the point meets the tail of the face mark. These marks are now critically important, because they identify a known flat face and a known flat edge that's also known to be 90° to the face. Now when you use a square, every time you put the square up against the piece, always put the body of the square up against either the marked face or the marked edge. You never want to put it up against one of the unmarked surfaces. That way you're always referencing off a known point, so that you don't have errors adding up to throw things out of square.

10

If your straightedge check shows you've rounded the board, mark a couple of lines within a couple inches of the ends. These are start and finish lines for scooping out a corrective cut between them. Set the plane on the edge with the iron at the start line. Plane across until the iron reaches the finish line and lift off. Do a couple passes until the iron is no longer cutting, because it's held up by the high points you've created at the ends. Then take one or two full-length cuts, until you've brought these high points down flat with the rest.

Achieving Width (W)

To plane the workpiece to width, the W step, mark the width on the board on the reference face, measured from the reference edge, parallel to that edge. Mount the workpiece in the vise with this edge up and the grain rising away from you. For a board with a lot of extra width, you can rip the excess off with a ripsaw. Otherwise, take it down close to the line with the #5 jack plane set for a heavy cut. Use full-length or diagonal nibbling strokes to quickly remove the excess. You can easily remove up to a half inch of material this way. Planing this edge is exactly the same as the reference edge, with the extra requirement that you are taking it down to a measured line, all along the length. Rough it down close to the line. Don't worry about how rough it is, all you care about is that you don't go past your line. If there are high spots, plane them selectively.

Once you are close to the line, switch to the #7 jointer plane. Start with the plane set for a heavy cut to take off the rough surface left by the jack plane, then dial it back as you get full shavings and approach the line. Check for square. You don't have to check with a straightedge, because you are working to the marked line. Finish the last passes with lighter shavings. If you have to make any corrections, make them while there is still extra margin to the width, otherwise you may reach the line before the edge is fully corrected. If you need to even up the distance from the line on some spots, you can use lifting cuts to plane just those areas, then follow with full-length strokes. Planing down to the line exactly is a precision operation for precise, square width.

Thicknessing (T)

To plane the workpiece to thickness, the T step, set a marking gauge to the desired thickness. Run it all along the edges and ends, referencing off the reference face by holding the fence against that face. Remember to tip the gauge so the pin or knife trails. It helps to run a pencil along the mark to make it more visible. This makes a uniform mark at a uniform thickness all around. Because you marked it off the reference face, which you know is flat, you know that it marks out a flat plane parallel to that face. So as long as you plane down to that mark uniformly, you know that this face will be flat and parallel to that face.

Planing this face is exactly the same as the reference face, with the extra requirement that you are taking it down to a measured line all around. With the #5 jack, take a couple of passes tipped to the side across the back edge to prevent spelching. You can take it down close to the line.

3

With the plane set for a heavy cut, take traversing passes across the grain. You can easily remove up to a ¼" of material this way. You'll get thick rolled-up pencil-sharpener shavings. Lean in as you extend the cut to get your whole body behind it. As you start to get close to the line, back off the depth of cut. You can constantly adjust the cut to deal with the conditions of the wood and the grain. Set it heavy for speed, but lighter to deal with difficulty. Anything you leave here you'll have to do with the flattening plane, which will take much lighter shavings.

4

Once you're within a heavy shaving of the line, switch to the #7 jointer. Turn the workpiece around if necessary to make sure you're going with the grain. Set for a heavy cut. The first couple of passes will just take off the high spots left by the jack plane. Once you start to get fuller shavings, start to back off the depth of cut. Remember the follow-through aim so you don't stop short. Plane in even, overlapping strokes to take the whole surface down to the line uniformly. Check for unevenness or high spots by running your fingers over the surface and checking with a straightedge. Do any corrections while you still have some margin above the line, and finish up with lighter shavings. Just like the width, planing down to the line exactly is a precision operation for precise, flat thickness. The only consideration is to leave enough extra thickness for final smoothing.

5

Finish up with the smoother set for very light shavings, taken in overlapping passes, or wait to do this step after assembly to do final clean up. This should only reduce the thickness by a hair.

If your vise has a dog hole or a lift-up dog, and you have dog holes lined up with it on the bench, this is an alternate setup you can use for lengthwise planing.

This allows you to get behind the work. It's still an upper body motion, lean and extend. This offers some different body mechanics that you might prefer.

For a workpiece that's longer than the depth of your workbench, use this alternate batten setup. The cross batten has a single dog that fits in a dog hole. It can pivot to butt up against angled workpiece ends. The second batten backs it up, held down with a holdfast.

Working from the end of the bench, this is another lean-and-extend motion, limited only by the depth of your reach.

Preparing the First End (E)

1

End grain is the hardest thing to plane. The stiff fibers of the wood resist cutting and will chip out if you go off the corner. It's also hard to keep the plane square because there's just a small bearing surface. For this, the secret precision weapon of hand tool woodworking is the shooting board. It has a hook on the front edge that catches up against the front edge of the bench, a fence or stop at the back for holding the workpiece, and a bed for guiding the plane. The plane rides sideways on the bed. There are many different designs. The key to a shooting board of any style is that the fence is precisely 90° to the bed. The fence on this one has a shimmable face that allows me to get it exactly 90° to the bed.

2

When using a shooting board, always place the reference edge of the workpiece up against the fence. That ensures that the shot corners will always be exactly 90° to that edge. Since the width edge is parallel to the reference edge, that ensures that the corners on that edge will also be exactly 90°. You can use any plane that has a side square to its bed for shooting. A large plane with heavy mass to carry it through the cut works well, but smaller planes also work, especially if they have a low-angle iron, such as bevel-up styes. There are also specialty shooting planes. The iron needs to be sharp to shear cleanly through the end grain. It also needs to be aligned parallel with the bed of the plane. Lubricate the bed and side of the plane with a scribble of wax or a wipe across an oil wick.

To plane the end, the second E step, scribe a line square across the board from the reference edge, close to the end. Since this corner will be the trailing corner when shooting, it can easily tear out as the plane passes by. To prevent this, nip off the corner. Turn the workpiece upside down and angle it on the shooting board so this corner is at the leading position, then plane across it on the shooting board. Alternatively, you can cut straight down across it with a chisel. Flip the workpiece over to butt the reference edge and this corner against the fence, the end overhanging the bed one shaving's worth.

Set the plane for a medium cut. You want to remove material as quickly as you can, but too heavy and it will be hard to plane across the end grain. Hold the workpiece tight up against the fence with your off hand. This also holds the shooting board tight against the front of the bench. Starting with the plane iron back from the leading corner of the workpiece so that you can build momentum to carry it through the cut, lean in and shoot it forward with a sharp impulse. Then just as with face planing, aim to finish the shot with the iron out past the fence, giving you follow-through. Hold the plane flat and square on the bed, running against the shooting board edge. This may take a bit of practice to coordinate. You should hear a tearing, schussing sound as the plane cuts across. Take repeated passes, advancing the workpiece overhanging the edge by one shaving at a time. Once you get past the uneven spots, the plane should produce continuous pencil-sharpener shavings. If you just get crumbly dust, sharpen the iron. If the plane repeatedly stops short in the middle of the cut, back off the iron a bit.

Check that the end is square to the reference face and square to the reference edge. If it isn't square to the face, you may have rocked the plane a bit as you shot it. You can also use the lateral adjustment of the plane to tip the iron a bit to one side or the other to compensate and reshoot it. If it isn't square to the face, you may not have held it well enough against the fence. Also check that the fence is square to the bed. This is a precision operation to get an accurate end that is square in two dimensions.

Trimming to Length (L)

1

2

To trim the workpiece to length, the L step, measure the length from the shot end and mark a line across the workpiece at that point. Unless there is just a small amount to remove, saw the excess off, leaving a little extra. The sawing does not need to be precise.

Saw this off with a crosscut saw and bench hooks. This is a third-class cut, because it's wide of the length measurement. It just needs to remove the excess, without worrying about appearance or accuracy.

3

Shoot the sawn edge down to the exact length. Set the reference edge against the fence and shoot this end the same as the first end, except that now you're working to a measured line. If the line is actually marked on the bottom side, transfer it around to the top side so you can see it. Sneak up on the length one shaving at a time and check for square in both dimensions. This is a precision operation that results in an end that is square and the exact length.

4 A

4 B

You can shoot with a low-angle block plane. **(A)** The low angle allows it to cut cleanly across end grain. The plane must have sides square to the body. **(B)** Cup your hand over the end of the plane, line up the tip with the near corner of the workpiece so you'll be able to build momentum, and take a shot that follows through past the far corner.

A well-shot end will allow a workpiece to stand upright with no rocking. This board has a jointed edge that was held against the shooting board fence.

6 A

6 B

(A) The board stands straight with the face square to the bench, and (B) the edge square to the bench.

A

B

(A) For larger workpieces too wide for your shooting board, you can plane end grain directly. Mount the workpiece end up in the vise. Use a shorter plane that's easier to manage, such as a #4. The plane needs to be very sharp, set for a light cut. Skew the plane to the cut, and plane in from the corner to the middle, lifting off. Turn the workpiece around in the vise and plane in from the second corner to meet the first cut in the middle, again lifting off. If the grain is hard to plane, tip the plane to each side to plane off the corners of the edges, leaving a narrower end grain ridge. Then plane flat across that ridge. This turns the full-width cut into three easier partial-width cuts. (B) The result is a crisp, square end that's as good as a shot end can be. Whether you use a shooting board or plane the end grain directly, a sharp, well-tuned handplane allows you to creep up on your final dimension one thin shaving at a time.

A common problem is rolling the plane from one side to the other as you go down the length of the cut. It's exaggerated here in the photo for illustration, but the plane starts tipped to the one side **(A)**, then ends up tipped to the other side **(B)**. The result is twist in the edge. Instead of being flat, it's shaped more like an airplane propeller. There's a gap one side at the near end of the board **(C)**, that turns into a gap on the other side at the far end **(D)**. The edge is only flat somewhere in the middle.

This situation is similar to when winding sticks reveal that the face of the board is in wind, or twisted. Just as in that case, the way to correct it is to plane from high point to high point. Holding the plane level, center and balance it over the high point at the near end **(A)**, and carefully plane down the edge in a long, narrow diagonal to end up centered over the far end high spot **(B)**. The shaving will start out skinny on one side, widen out, and taper back to skinny on the other side. It may take several passes this way to eliminate the twist. Concentrate on keeping the plane level through the cut. It helps to use a light cut and keep your arms close to your body, stepping through the cut rather than pushing through it with your arms. Finish up with a regular full-width shaving.

Sometimes you have a long, thin workpiece that needs edge planing. It's too flexible to hold in the vise, because it will bow at the far end or in the middle.

One solution is to raise the planing stop in the bench and butt the end of the workpiece against it. That leaves the entire length of the workpiece supported on the bench (**A**). You can also use this for wider workpieces (**B**), raising the stop up higher. However, since the workpiece is just resting loosely against the stop, it may slide around.

To stabilize these workpieces, use a bird's-mouth jig. There are a variety of different styles. This one is the most basic, knocked together from scraps.

Secure the upright keel of the jig in the vise, then wedge the work into place in the notch. Now the workpiece is gripped at the end so it doesn't slide around, and fully supported by the bench. This works for narrow workpieces (**A**), and wider ones (**B**).

The force of planing simply drives the workpiece tighter into the mouth. Use a softer wood for the jig, so that the mouth doesn't dent the end of the workpiece.

Using Wooden Handplanes

If you're using wooden handplanes, the process is the same. Set the cut to the same depth as the corresponding metal plane, adjusting as necessary for speed control. Lubricate the bottom, and use the same upper body motion to lean into the cut. Start off with the midsize wooden jack plane. Grip the tote with the usual trigger-finger grip. Note the front handgrip **(A)** with your thumb on the near side of the plane. You can set the iron for an aggressive cut and use a diagonal nibbling action **(B)** for heavy stock removal.

Follow up with the long wooden jointer plane for flattening. Here the front handgrip is similar to a metal plane, with your fingers curled underneath as a guide.

Finish up with the short wooden smoothing plane. This style is known as a "coffin smoother," not because it's used for smoothing coffins, but because of its coffin shape.

One final type of plane useful for heavy roughing is a scrub plane. This is a short, narrow plane, with a tightly cambered iron. That allows you to set it for a deep, narrow chip.

Take a heavy shaving off the back edge to avoid spelching, then traverse across the grain. The narrow curved iron peels up narrow shavings. Take overlapping passes to rough the whole surface down evenly. You can also use diagonal passes. This works just as well on edges, where the diagonal nibbling pattern is effective with the heavy cut.

PLANING EXERCISE

This exercise will help you develop control of the planes. As with the rough sawing practice, work out any problems on cheap practice lumber before you try it on good lumber. Then practice on some hardwood.

Use the depth adjustment as your speed control. It's like the gearshift on your car. You don't just leave it set in one gear the whole time. You're constantly shifting up and down for heavier or lighter cut, to go faster or slower.

Use the trigger-finger grip, and lubricate your plane with a scribble of wax or a swipe on an oil wick.

This is also a good opportunity to look at some different workholding setups and try out some different planes.

1

For face-planing longer workpieces, there are several ways to secure the work, depending on how your workbench is set up. If it has an end vise, clamp the workpiece flat, butted up against a bench dog on one end and the vise dog on the other end. This bench has a planing stop and dog holes. Raise the stop high enough to catch the workpiece, but below the level you'll be planing.

2

Butt the end of the workpiece against the stop. Place a dog or other stop in the dog hole nearest the other end. If using a plain dog, use a wedge or a pair of opposing wedges to jam the workpiece up securely. This stop is a Wonder Dog. It acts as a mini end vise in a dog hole. Whatever method you use, don't over-tighten. That can cause the workpiece to bow upward.

3

Run the jack plane down the back edge to take a shaving off the corner to prevent spelching, then traverse straight across the board, here using a wooden jack. Skewing the plane may help the cut if it is tearing out too roughly. This board is slightly cupped, so the plane initially takes shavings off the near and far edges, leaving the middle untouched.

Take repeated passes, here using a metal jack. Once the high edges are down even with the middle, the plane will start taking full-length shavings. Check the board with winding sticks to make sure you get it generally flat, planing the high spots to get them down level with the low spots. The planes you use for this roughing step don't need to be your finest planes. Old beat-up planes work just fine. Save the fine planes for the fine steps.

If your workbench doesn't have a built-in stop, you can butt the workpiece up against a wooden or brass bench dog. These are softer material so that if you run your plane into them, you won't damage it.

On the other, use a doe's foot (A). This is simply a board with a 90° notch in the end. With the board stopped at the other end against something, push the notch against the workpiece and secure it to the workbench with a holdfast or clamp.

Switch over to the jointer plane. Start with diagonal passes to clean up the rough surface left by the jack, with the jointer set for relatively heavy shavings. Check with winding sticks and plane any high spots down selectively.

A board that's cupped like this will rock under the plane. To eliminate that, flip the board over and take straight strokes down the middle with the jack plane. Don't traverse across the grain, because the plane will tend to follow the rocker rather than remove it. Once you've removed enough to make it lie still, flip it back over.

9

10

Change over to straight, full-length strokes with the jointer, taking overlapping passes. Work in an orderly fashion across the surface of the board to keep it at a consistent flatness. Back off the iron for finer shavings as you approach your final surface. For additional practice, rough the surface down again with the jack plane and reflatten it with the jointer.

To practice edge-planing, mount the workpiece edge-up in the front vise. Support the other end so it doesn't slip down as you work.

11 A

11 B

Using different planes, try taking straight strokes **(A)**, and skewed strokes **(B)** down the full length of the workpiece. Try with different depths of cut. Try tipping the plane over to bevel off the edge, then flatten back out to return it to square. With the jack plane, try diagonal nibbling strokes. The goal here is as much to get a general feel for the tools as it is to practice squaring an edge. Repeatedly square it up, then rough it down. Try deliberately producing a poor edge, then correcting it. Turning an entire board into a pile of shavings is an excellent way to develop control.

12

To practice end-grain planing, mark a couple of lines across the end, about 1/16" apart.

13 A

13 B

Mount the piece end-up in the vise. With a sharp, fine-set smoother **(A)** plane down to the first line. Spin the workpiece around **(B)** so that you come in from both corners to the middle. Try both straight and skewed cuts.

14

With a sharp, fine-set low-angle block plane, repeat this to plane down to the second line.

15

While you have a block plane out, chamfering is another fun exercise. Start with the end grain. Mark guide lines on the end and face, and connect them with an angled line on the edge.

16 A

16 B

Hold the block plane skewed to the edge, and tilted at the chamfer angle. Running your fingers along the wood as guides, come in from both sides to the middle. Block planes are great for this kind of work, because of the way they fit in the hand.

17

Do the same on the long-grain edge, again running your fingers as guides along the wood. In addition to chamfers, you can form any kind of convex roundover on end-grain and long-grain edges, such as quarter-round, half-round or bullnose.

18

By the time you're done, you'll have created a cloud of different shavings. These make great tinder for your fireplace or campfire.

TAPERING

The FEWTEL sequence produces a nice workpiece with parallel faces in all dimensions. But what if what you want is a tapered workpiece, for instance for table legs?

1

A squared-up leg blank marked on two sides for a compound tapered table leg. One way to do this is by resawing. But it's easy to do with handplanes.

2

Start with a #5 jack plane to rough down the bulk of the material. Set the plane for a heavy cut, and hold it at a skewed angle. First work on the thickest portion of the tapered waste, about a third of the way from the far end of the workpiece. As you get this down parallel to the marked line, start working your way backward with each successive stroke.

3

Keep working a roughly parallel surface until you're within one heavy shaving of the line. The surface will be scalloped from the cambered jack plane iron.

4

Switch to the #7 jointer plane, set for a heavy cut initially. The first few strokes will nip off the high points of the scalloped surface. Get the entire surface parrallel to the line, selectively taking a shaving off the high sections until it's even. As it starts to take full shavings, back off the iron. Check for square and flatness. Finish the last few strokes with light cuts. This leg has a straight, non-tapered portion at the top, so be careful not to plane past that transition line. It needs to match up with the transition on the next side of the leg.

5

Mark the line on the tapered face and rotate the leg to the next side to taper. This presents a problem for clamping, since the tapered face is no longer parallel to the vise. One solution is to put a scrap in the gap so the vise can apply even pressure.

6

Another solution is to butt it up against the planing stop and put a backing batten behind it with holdfasts. Make sure the stop and holdfasts are clear of the plane path.

7

Rough it down like the first face, then switch over to the jointer.

8

The nose of my long jointer started hitting the bench at this angle, so I switched back to the vise to finish up.

9

The completed tapered leg. This process works for tapering any number of sides, as well as for hexagonal or octagonal legs.

Use Wedges to Improve Workholding

You can improve the workholding by making long wedges. Mark out a workpiece to resaw. Start on a long side. Resawing on an angle is no different from resawing straight down the length.

Stand the workpiece up on end in the vise and saw down the length. Then turn it to the other long side and repeat the sawing steps.

The wedge fits in the vise with the tapered leg better than the scrap. Making the wedges takes a little more time, but they can be useful for other setups. This is how you build up a creative collection of jigs to handle odd situations, one project at a time.

Using the wedges on the bench, with a Wonder Dog applying pressure to the leg against the stop. The wedges underneath raise the tapered section up parallel to the bench, so now the jointer can travel clear across it.

PANEL RAISING

Raised panels are used in frame-and-panel construction. You can make them using specialty planes with irons shaped to form the chamfer and edge, called "badger planes," but there are a variety of methods using more general-purpose tools.

Left, pillow-style panel, with a simple chamfered edge all around. Right, raised-field panel, with the additional complexity of lowering the edges of the field along the chamfer.

The panel floats loose in a grooved frame. This compensates for wood movement, allowing the panel to expand and contract freely due to changes in humidity.

Making a Pillow-style Panel

1

To make a pillow-style panel, start with a squared-up workpiece. The tools are a combination square set for 1½", a marking gauge set for ¼", a chisel for relieving the corners, a #5 jack plane for roughing, a #4 smoothing plane for final chamfering, and holdfasts to secure the panel. Use a pencil for marking so you don't leave marks in the surface. Make sure the planes are sharp and soles lubricated.

2

Using the combination square as a depth gauge, mark the distance 1½" from all four edges.

3

Slide the blade of the square out and use it as a straightedge to draw lines at those distances. This marks out the chamfers on the top.

4

Using the marking gauge, scribe all the way around the edges, registering off the back of the workpiece. This marks out all the chamfers on the edges. I've drawn exaggerated grain lines on the side to show which way the grain is rising on the long edges.

5

Secure the workpiece in the vise and use the chisel to relieve the corners. This is a rough operation, removing chips to take it down near the scribed line. This prevents tear-out when you plane across the grain for the end chamfers.

6

Secure the workpiece to the bench with holdfasts and a batten. With the #5 jack plane set for a heavy cut, hold it at a skewed angle and pitched over the end corner. Plane across to rough out the end chamfer.

7

Take it down close to the lines on top and edge, but leave some margin to correct any error. In addition to skewed cuts across the grain, you can plane at an angle or directly down the slope of the chamfer, especially if you have worked selectively on spots to even them out. Try different stroke directions and different skew angles to see how the grain responds.

8

Complete the chamfer with the #4 smoother, set initially for a heavy cut. Try different angles of skew and cut to see which produces the best surface. You want a clean, shearing cut. Plane selectively to bring down the high spots. As you get down to the line, back off the depth of cut and concentrate on maintaining the chamfer angle consistently across the surface with smooth, full strokes. The last shaving should just make the line disappear on the surface. Turn the workpiece to the other end and repeat the process.

9

Check the fit of the edge in the groove using a mullet. This is a short section of stock grooved to the same dimensions as your frame. The easiest way to make it is to make one of your frame sections a few inches longer, then cut off the excess to use as the mullet. The priority is to make the top of the chamfer look good. If you go a little thinner down on the edge, that's not a problem, because it will be held in a groove.

10

Orient the workpiece to work on the first long-grain edge. Repeat the process with the jack and smoothing planes. The work will go much faster in this long-grain orientation. Skewing the plane may still help, but may not be necessary.

11

The challenge is to make the ridge where the chamfers meet straight and crisp at each corner, while meeting the line on the top and the mark on the side. Everything needs to meet up at once in multiple dimensions. You may need to take a thin corrective shaving on the upper or lower portion of the chamfer, then take additional passes to grow it wider and wider until it meets the other edge. There's a lot of visual geometry in this. It only takes one shaving too far to ruin it.

12

The grain orientation on the last side presents a problem on the bench top. One solution is to plane in the opposite direction. But another solution is to mount this edge-up in the vise. Instead of planing from the top side, plane from the front face. Rough it down with the #5.

13

Finish with the #4. It may help to angle the workpiece in the vise to deal with awkward grain direction.

14

Because there's no raised field on this panel, you can easily use a scraper for any final cleanup.

15

To scrape the cross-grain facets, angle the scraper and go diagonally across to the edge.

16

You can also scrape it secured on the bench top.

17

Scrape the last of the top surface pencil marks.

18

The completed panel, with four crisp ridges where the facets meet.

Making a Raised-field Panel

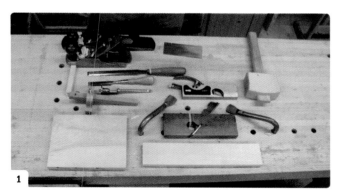

1

To make a raised-field panel, most of the tools are the same. Instead of a combination square use a cutting gauge. You need something to lower the edge next to the field. This can be a paring chisel, a shoulder plane or a skew rabbet plane. The clamping batten lower right is actually a guide piece. It has a jointed edge with a reference mark that will act as a fence for these tools.

2

Using the cutting gauge set to 1½", mark the top surface all around. This replaces the pencil lines from the pillow style. The cutter is actually what's forming the shoulders of the field, making the initial surface cuts to the desired depth with several repeated passes. If you're having difficulty getting the proper depth when working in a harder wood, you can run a saw along those lines very carefully.

Use a gauge set to ¼" to mark the edges, registered from the back.

Relieve the corners with a bench chisel.

Rough the end chamfer with the #5 jack. This time, though, stay farther away from the marked line on the top surface. That's where you'll lower the surface to leave the raised field.

Scribe some lines across the grain in this area with a marking knife. This weakens the grain so that it will peel up easily.

Deepen the shoulder if you need to with the cutting gauge.

Run the paring chisel flat across to roll up the surface grain. Be very careful not to run the chisel into the field edge. That's a very visible feature, so any flaw will be apparent.

9

Pare across almost to the far edge, but not over it, to avoid tear-out. Push on the handle, but drive it with your thumb on the end. That provides careful steering and careful application of force.

10

Come in from the other side toward the middle. Use your fingers on the end for drive, steering and control. Go back and forth to step the edge down a layer at a time. If you pare deeper than the gauge line, raising some feathers that are still attached, trim them off with the cutting gauge.

11

Plane across, first with the #5 if there's a lot of material left, then with the smoother. Be very careful along the field edge so you don't damage it. Since the plane won't reach all the way up to the edge, you'll clean that up separately.

12

Pare across lightly with the paring chisel to take down the flat along the edge, coming in from both sides to the middle.

13

This will produce a new ridge. Plane that down with the smoother. Repeat this alternation of chisel and smoother until the entire surface forms a flat chamfer from the raised field to the outer edge.

14

On the long-grain side, starting with the #5.

15

With the paring chisel, curl up the flat along the field. This is a very delicate edge. Be careful about running the corner of the chisel into it. Once you've formed an initial shoulder, use that to guide the chisel along.

16

Reverse the chisel to pare down the other end. Since this is against the grain, just take a very light shaving.

17

Repeat the alternating process of plane and chisel to eliminate the ridge while meeting the adjacent chamfer at the corner.

18

You can use a scraper to even out the surface and eliminate the last whisper of ridge. The scraper works either direction, with or against the grain. Run the corner of the scraper lightly in the shoulder of the field.

Panel Raising: Alternate Approaches

The chisel provided the least control for lowering the edge along the field. For more control, after roughing down the end, secure a jointed batten aligned to the top scribe line to use as a fence. Run a skew rabbet plane along that to quickly take shavings down. The fence keeps it from running into the edge, and the bed of the plane keeps it from diving in unevenly. You can run a marking knife across the top surface first to weaken the grain as before.

A shoulder plane is another good choice, though it will generally be a little slower because it takes finer shavings. Both of these planes have irons that go all the way to the side of the plane, allowing them to get right into the shoulder of the field.

Both of these planes produce a ridge the same as the chisel did. Follow up with the #4 smoother.

Alternate with the shoulder plane pitched over. The shoulder plane is better for this than the rabbet plane because it takes finer shavings.

Do the long-grain edge the same way. Rough it down with the #5, then use the rabbet or shoulder plane, alternating with the #4. This particular workpiece allowed me to plane both long edges in the same direction. If you need to plane the other direction, you can mount it edge up in the vise.

If you are a little shy of the line along the edge of the field, you can lay either the rabbet or shoulder plane on its side and run it down that edge to trim it exactly. Be careful doing this across the grain to avoid tear-out.

To scrape the end chamfers, lay the scraper across and go straight down the surface.

Another excellent method uses these skew block planes, in right- and left-hand versions. The planes are wide enough to cut the entire chamfer, and have a fence that rides along the edge to control the width. They have a nicker to sever the fibers in cross-grain cuts. The removable side allows the iron to get right into the shoulder. The bevel-up iron is bedded at a low angle and skewed across the mouth. The combination of bed angle and skew makes them work equally well along the grain, across the grain, and on end grain. They perform as well as dedicated badger planes, yet are still general-purpose enough for other tasks. The right and left versions allow them to tackle long grain on either side of a workpiece.

Rough the chamfers out as with the other methods, or you can do the entire process with the skew block planes. They're surprisingly fast and efficient. Set the fence to the width of the chamfer, accounting for its angle; this is wider than just the flat width on the surface, because it is the hypotenuse of a right triangle. Holding the fence tight against the end, with the plane pitched over at the chamfer angle, plane across. The fence also has screw holes to allow you to screw an angled wooden fence to it to set the pitch angle for the chamfer.

The long-grain orientation. This is with the right-handed plane, where the fence is on the left side.

The long grain on the other side. Hold the workpiece edge-up in the vise. This is with the left-handed plane, where the fence is on the right side.

This alternative setup allows you to plane the second long-grain side flat on the bench, using a large planing board. There's a scrap underneath the edge of the board to raise it up a bit so the fence of the plane doesn't hit the bench. This setup will work for the cross-grain chamfers as well.

CHAPTER 4
SIMPLE JOINERY

GRAIN & STRENGTH

Grain orientation is one of the main characteristics that defines the strength of wood and joints. Good joinery takes these factors into account, resulting in workmanship that will last for centuries. Poor joinery results in projects that fall apart in a couple of years.

These two pieces of pine are identical size, both from the same board. In the rear piece, the grain runs along the length, known as "long grain." In the front piece, the grain runs along the width. Because this is a short distance, it's known as "short grain."

Short grain is very weak. It breaks apart easily. It can't take any force, and provides no structural strength. This snapped easily in my hands.

Long grain is very strong. It can withstand enormous force, and provides tremendous structural strength. This workpiece only dented and bounced when hammered on with a mallet. However, it splits easily along the grain with a wedge.

Long-grain edge-glued joints are very strong as long as the edges are planed flat and smooth, known as "jointing." With modern glues, they are often stronger than the wood itself. This is a common method of gluing up workpieces to make wide panels. The glue bonds the fibers all along their length.

Long-grain face-glued joints are also very strong. The faces need to be planed flat and smooth. This is a common method of gluing up workpieces to make thick laminations. As with edge-glued joints, the glue bonds the fibers all along their length.

Cross-grain face- or edge-glued joints are weak, because the glue doesn't bond along the length of the fibers.

End-grain to edge-grain glued joints are extremely weak. Glue just soaks into end grain. The tips of the fibers bond weakly to the long-grain fibers.

End-grain to end-grain is just as weak.

Workpieces that need to be joined together at an angle or at an end need some kind of mechanical structure for strength, such as this mortise-and-tenon. The tenon fits in the mortise and is glued or pegged, forming a very strong joint. Dovetails are another very strong mechanical structure.

The other critical characteristic of grain is wood movement. Wood is like a sponge, constantly absorbing and releasing moisture. That causes it to expand and contract in width, across the grain. Even wood that's decades old will do this. It won't move in length, along the grain. Every wood is a little different, but the amount of movement is proportional to the width of the workpiece. So if the wood expands and contracts by 5 percent over time, the narrow workpiece on the left will have a much smaller absolute change than the wider one.

USING THE CHISEL

Chisels are incredibly versatile joinery tools that are often under used. A number of more specialized tools are simply a replacement for a chisel method in order to provide more control (a handplane being the most obvious example – a plane iron is like a very thin, wide chisel with the plane body providing control). That means if you don't have that specialized tool, you can still do the job, using a chisel freehand.

There are many different types of chisels for different operations, with different shapes and handle types, made in a range of widths. Some are made for heavy use, such as chopping mortises, where you may drive them with a mal-let. Others are made for lighter, more delicate use, such as paring, where you drive them only with hand pressure.

The bench chisels are the most versatile, a compromise of the different characteristics. They can be used for everything from light paring to heavier chopping. Their handles are strong enough that they can be used with a mallet.

Try exercises here with each of your chisels, paying attention to which ones are made for a mallet and which ones aren't. Try some cross-grain orientation, some splitting, some shaving, some bevel-up, some bevel-down, some paring, some chopping. See how they respond to different soft and hard woods.

A range of chisel types, from the lightest paring chisel up to the heaviest mortising chisel. These are the types you'll find most commonly. From left, antique paring chisel, antique socket bench chisel, modern premium socket bench chisel, modern sash mortise chisel and antique oval bolstered mortise chisel.

An antique paring chisel, sharpened at 20°-25°. This is a long, thin chisel for delicate work. It has a light, thin tang for the handle, so you would never use a mallet on this, only hand pressure.

An antique socket bench chisel. This is also long, but thicker than the paring chisel, sharpened at 30° for general bench work. The heavy socket allows you to use it with a mallet. The end of the handle has a leather washer to keep it from splitting.

A modern high-quality premium socket bench chisel similar to the antique one, but shorter. The sides of all these chisels are beveled to allow them to work inside the spaces of joints, such as inside dovetails. There are also non-beveled chisels called "firmer" chisels.

A modern mortising chisel, sharpened at an angle of 30°-35°. This is a lighter duty chisel than the oval bolstered one because of its thinner neck here. This is also known as a "sash mortise" chisel.

An oval bolstered mortise chisel, also known as a "pig sticker" because it looks like a vicious weapon. This can take the heaviest pounding in the heaviest wood. It is also sharpened somewhere between 30° and 35°. The cross section of these chisels is actually slightly trapezoidal. The top face of the chisel is a bit narrower so that the sides won't get jammed against the walls of a mortise.

  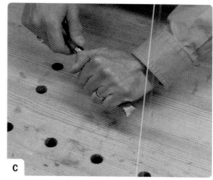

The safest way to handle a chisel is to have both hands on it – one hand on the handle, one hand somewhere on the body of the tool. Never put a hand in front of the chisel or in the cutting path, and never have any part of your body in the cutting path, including the path it might take if the tool slips. Your front hand often serves as a guide on the chisel. **(A)** An underhand grip. **(B)** Choked up close to the end to limit the depth of cut. **(C)** An overhand grip, which works bevel-up or bevel-down. These positions all keep the hands behind the cutting edge.

The handles on socket chisels can be replaced if they get beat up over time. **(A)** To remove a handle, hold the chisel flat and tap the handle on the bench as you turn it. **(B)** The handle loosens and slips out. **(C)** To seat a handle, hold the chisel upside down and tap the handle on the bench until it's firm. Don't glue it in place.

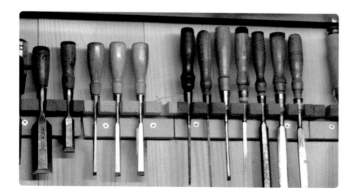

Hang socket chisels by their socket neck, not by their handles, so they don't slip out of their handles. Remember this when picking up a chisel as well. Tap it up tight if it's loose. Some of these handles have leather rings or metal hoops to protect the ends.

General Chisel Usage

A

B

Chamfering with the chisel, using the fingers as a guide, similar to jointing an edge with a handplane, with the chisel skewed for a delicate cut. **(A)** Take off the initial corner. **(B)** Once you've established a flat, register the back of the chisel along it to take curling shavings, using the skew angle to control the depth of cut.

A

B

C

Shaping a corner to a flat or convex profile. The free hand is an overhand grip, and the hand on the handle provides the drive. **(A)** Start flat. **(B)** Raise the handle to angle the cut down as you progress. **(C)** Rotate the chisel to chamfer the edge of the cut. You can alternate chamfering with flat cuts to remove the waste quickly.

Body mechanics doing this are similar to using a handplane. Lean your body into it, getting your upper body mass on the long lever of your legs behind the chisel, with your hands guiding it. Your arm position changes very little.

This produces a lovely variety of curls, shavings, and chips all from the same tool. These are good exercises to do on softwoods and hardwoods to get a feel for the resistance of the chisel and develop control.

With bevel-up orientation the chisel may may dive too deep. Bevel-down orientation gives you more depth control. (A) Bevel-up, the chisel dives in quickly. (B) Bevel-down, you can lower the handle to lever the cutting edge up, reducing the depth of cut. This is also useful for levering out a chip.

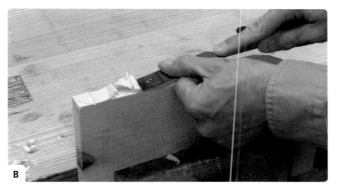

You can use bevel-up orientation to scoop out concave sections. (A) Start with the handle high. (B) Lower the handle as you come across to complete the scooping action.

Always cut downhill across the gain. **(A)** Come in from the left down across the grain to the lowest point. **(B)** Come in from the right to meet the left cut. Alternate from each side until you've carved out the entire curve. Be careful about levering out too heavy a chip at one time, which might cause it to follow the grain in a direction you don't want it to go.

You can alternate bevel-down and bevel-up for rough and fine work. **(A)** Bevel-down, take deep diving cuts and lever back out to rough out an edge. **(B)** Bevel-up, choked up on the end, skewing the chisel, and registering its flat back on the surface, clean up the resulting scalloped edge to level it out.

The chisel works nicely on cross grain, again by skewing it and using your fingers as a guide as you zip sideways. Just like using a block plane to bevel an edge, you can do it with the chisel.

Another cross-grain usage is cleaning out dados between scribed and sawn lines. **(A)** Roll up the grain bevel-up. **(B)** Use the chisel bevel-down to go deeper and lever out, or if the dado is too long for the chisel bevel-up.

Using the Mallet & Chisel

Use a mallet when you need more force, such as in heavier wood or when chopping across grain. The mallet also allows you to make a precise application of force, providing controlled impulses with repeated small taps.

By varying the angle of the chisel and the force of the taps, you can go around convex curves.

The mallet is also very useful bevel-down, such as scooping out a concave curve. **(A)** Take light taps to precisely scoop out from one side. **(B)** Repeat from the other side to meet in the middle. A simple flat chisel is able to do both convex and concave shaping.

Chopping down across grain is a common operation. The wedging action of the chisel bevel will push out a chunk. This is another useful exercise to try in softwoods and hardwoods.

After chopping out heavy sections with the mallet, you can follow up with hand pressure for fine cleanup, paring down across the grain. Use one hand as a guide, and press down with your upper body. Just as the handplane is a whole-body tool, the chisel can also be a whole-body tool, putting your whole body mass behind it.

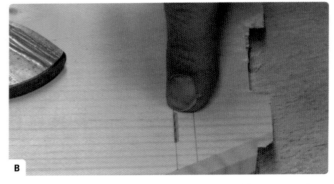

The wedging action of the bevel can cause the chisel to push back behind a line. **(A)** Set the chisel exactly on a pencil line across the grain, and strike heavily with the mallet. **(B)** The resulting cut has pushed just a hair back past the line.

This can happen in a scribed knife line as well. **(A)** Set the chisel exactly in a scribed line across the grain and strike heavily. **(B)** The resulting cut has pushed behind the line. This will result in a noticeable gap in joinery.

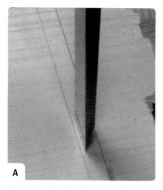

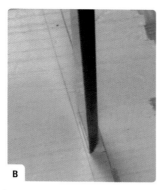

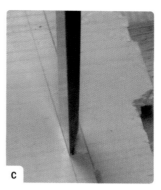

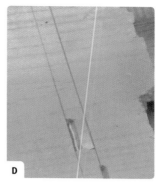

Prevent this by first making a relief chop away from the line so there's very little material to push against the wedge of the bevel, then trim exactly on the line. **(A)** Set the chisel away from the pencil, **(B)** strike heavily, **(C)** then set it right on the line and strike lightly or pare down with hand pressure, **(D)** leaving a cut exactly on the line. Since there's very little wood resisting the wedge of the bevel, the chisel doesn't get pushed back. Instead, the bevel pushes the thin wood back toward the relief cut.

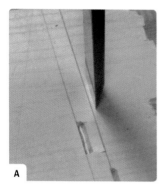

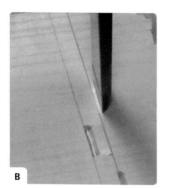

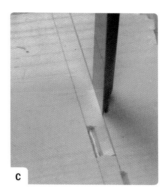

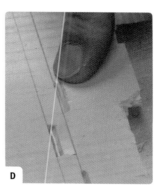

This works with the scribed line as well. **(A)** Set the chisel away from the line, **(B)** strike heavily, **(C)** then set it in the scribed line so it clicks into place and strike lightly or pare down with hand pressure, **(D)** leaving a cut exactly on the line.

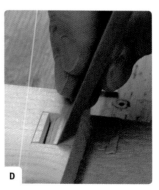

You can extend this strategy to make progressively deeper relief cuts to completely remove the bulk of the waste, then pare away the remainder in a couple of precise steps. This is also useful for harder wood. **(A)** Make the first chop away from the line. **(B)** Make a second angled cut behind that to remove a chip. **(C)** Deepen the first cut. **(D)** Remove an additional chip. Repeat this until you get all way through and the chunk of waste pops off.

(A) Make the first paring cut half the thickness of the remainder. **(B)** Make the final paring exactly on the line. **(C)** The completed cut.

When making a series of cross-grain chops, for instance for a mortise or to make a shallow recess, the direction the bevel faces relative to the direction of advance will produce different chips, as does the angle of the chisel. **(A)** The bevel forward as it advances, the wedging action pushing the chisel and wood backwards, going deeper as it goes forward. Use this orientation to go deep. **(B)** The bevel backward as it advances, there's much less wedging action, so the chips don't move much and the chisel doesn't go as deep. Use this orientation to keep it shallow.

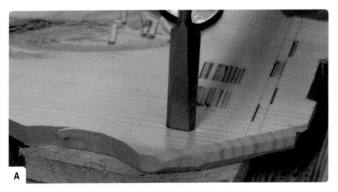

Chiseling along the grain has much more dramatic effect. **(A)** The chisel goes in deep immediately when struck. **(B)** A second chisel cut next to the first splits a large piece off.

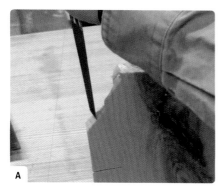  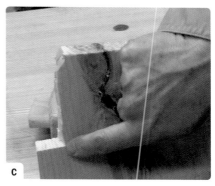

Uncontrolled splitting can ruin a workpiece, but controlled splitting is a quick way to hog off waste. **(A)** With a stop cut running across the grain below, take the first split down the grain well away from the line so you can see what the grain is going to do. **(B)** Continue splitting off a chunk at a time, making each one smaller as you approach the line. **(C)** The finished cut is very rough.

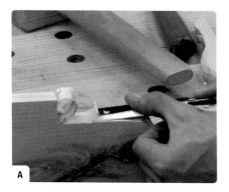  

(A) Pare across to clean up the cut, taking light parings to avoid diving deeply. **(B)** Chop the parings off inside the corner. **(C)** The finished cut is now smooth, straight, square and precise.

Use stop cuts to limit how far chips split off. **(A)** A stop cut across the grain at the low point of a notch. **(B)** Chiseling from the right, the chips stop at the stop cut. **(C)** From the left to complete the notch. Use bevel-up orientation to make straight cuts, or bevel-down orientation with a scooping motion to make curved cuts.

  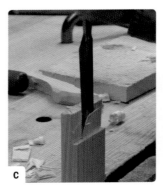 

You can use this method to split off tenon cheeks if the grain is straight. **(A)** After cutting the shoulder line as a stop cut, **(B)** make the first split half the thickness of the cheek so you can see what the grain is going to do. Continue this all the way across. **(C)** Make the next layer of splits half the remaining thickness. **(D)** Remove the final layers with careful parings.

 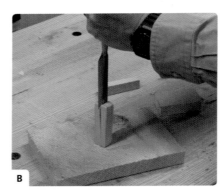 

Make pegs for pinning joints by splitting them out. The full-length grain will be very strong. **(A)** Split squares off a short piece of straight-grained stock. **(B)** Split the square across its thickness. This will follow the grain, showing the true side of the peg. **(C)** Split the splits.

Point the pegs with the chisel on a bench hook. You can use them square or drive them through a dowel plate. This works with all kinds of woods, taking advantage of the relative strengths and weaknesses in the different directions of the grain.

Use a paring chisel for final cleanup. Drive and steer it with your thumb and fingers, using your hand at the back for added power as you register the flat back on the surface. In addition to straight and skewed cuts across the grain, sideways shearing, slicing and circular motions take precise, delicate shavings.

An oval bolstered pig-sticker mortise chisel can take heavy pounding. It chops deeply into the wood, and the thick body allows you to lever out large chunks without snapping. This is especially useful in heavy wood such as oak.

EDGE JOINTS

Structurally, an edge-glued joint is the simplest joint there is, because it's literally just two long grain edges glued together, no mechanical support. This is the only joint where we can rely strictly on the glue, because modern glues will actually produce a joint here that's stronger than the wood itself.

1

Two workpieces prepared for edge gluing, marked with a reference face and a reference edge. You'll glue them on the mated reference edges that have been jointed flat, smooth and square. The arrows show how the grain is rising in the same direction once the opposing edges are brought together. That means you'll be able to plane the joined assembly as one in the same direction.

2

Check across the joint for flat using a straightedge. Even though both workpieces have been jointed independently, and the edges are 90° to the faces, minor variations and errors will add up. These two workpieces are just slightly out of flat when put together.

3

Rejoint one edge with a few corrective shavings so that the resultant joint is flat across both workpieces. Recheck for flatness and correct a little at a time to avoid over-correcting.

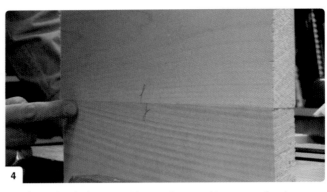

4

Dry fit to check the joint. The goal is to achieve a perfectly smooth line where everything joins together, with no gaps. That makes a strong glue joint.

5

To check for gaps, hold the workpieces together up to the light. There should be no light coming through along the joint.

6

Mark the workpieces with a cabinetmaker's triangle so you know how they go together. That's a triangle across a joint where the tip points to the top or front. That way if things get moved around, you know exactly how they go back together.

7

Set your clamps up, getting the spacing and opening prepared before you apply any glue. Stand the workpieces up in them, run a light bead of glue down each edge, and spread it with your fingertip so the entire edges are coated. Lay the workpieces down, rub the edges together to ensure good contact, and get them lined up flush.

8

Tighten the clamps and check for flatness, to make sure the workpieces don't buckle or slip out of alignment. Look for a little bit of even squeeze-out of glue. Don't overtighten the clamps, which can starve the joint of glue. You just need firm, even pressure. Some people like to clean up the squeeze-out immediately with a damp cloth or sponge, some like to let it dry partially and remove the rubbery glue, and some let it harden completely and then scrape it off.

After the glue has dried, scrape off any dried glue with a card scraper on each side.

Plane the panel down flush.

The result should be a perfectly smooth, seamless joint.

Testing the statement that the joint is stronger than the wood itself. This is holding 90 lbs. The wood is deflecting but the joint is holding up.

Try Gang-planing Your Boards

Another way to get the boards to line up flat is to gang-plane the edges together. Hold the two workpieces together in the vise and plane the edge. It doesn't matter if you plane perfectly square across, but make sure that you plane consistently across.

The matched edges don't have to be square, because the angles will offset each other.

3

4

Through the magic of geometry, when you unfold these workpieces and stand them on the planed edges, they form a perfectly flat 180° surface. That's because of complementary angles. One is a little higher than 90°, the other is a little lower than 90°, but they offset each other exactly so that when you add them up you get 180°.

Glue these up the same way. The only difference that the off-square joint makes is that you need to make sure one workpiece doesn't slide up past the other as you tighten the clamps. Scrape and plane the same way after the glue dries.

One consideration when gluing up panels is how they move with seasonal changes. I've highlighted the orientation of the rings in the end grain of these workpieces, as well as marked the direction they need to be planed. Orient boards like this with alternating up and down ring orientation, alternating the smiles and frowns in the ends. If all the boards have the same orientation and they start to cup individually, the overall panel will cup noticeably. Alternating them causes the different directions of cupping to effectively cancel out, maintaining an overall flat panel. Once you've figured out the appropriate orientations, mark lines across the joints so you can tell how to match them up during gluing.

Use a Spring Joint to Avoid Gaps

1

2

A common problem when gluing up long, narrow workpieces is gaps, or open joints, at the ends. Avoid this with a spring joint (also known as a sprung joint). If you put a straightedge along the jointed edge and twist it back and forth, you'll see where it rubs. If it rubs somewhere in the middle, the workpiece is slightly crowned. If it rubs on the ends, it's slightly concave. If you glue up a crowned edge, it will be open at one or both ends. Springing closes this up by deliberately making a slight concavity in the length, then clamping across it to flex the boards together sideways.

Take one or two stopped shavings, starting an inch or two from the near end of the board and finishing an inch or two from the far end. Check with the straightedge and the matching board to verify there's no pivot point between the ends.

When you set the boards together at this edge, only the ends will be in contact.

This leaves a very small gap in the center of the joint.

Check with a dry fit. Clamp the workpieces together roughly in the center third. Sometimes a single clamp in the center is sufficient.

Tighten the clamps and verify that they close up the joint.

Remove the clamps and get them ready for glue-up. Apply a light bead of glue to each edge and spread it with your fingertip.

Tighten the clamps, making sure everything is flush and flat. Check the ends and along the length to verify the entire joint is closed up, with uniform squeeze-out.

9

Clean up glue drops on your bench. If you leave them, they can damage freshly planed boards. Sprinkle some sawdust on them to absorb the moisture and let them dry for a minute, then use a card scraper to lightly scrape them off.

10

After the spring joint has dried, scrape each side.

11

Plane each side with the jointer.

12

Finish up with the smoother.

13

The result is a smooth, gap-free joint along the entire length and at the ends.

BOOKMATCHED JOINTS

Another type of edge glued joint is the bookmatched joint. This is useful for making up thin panels, such as for musical instrument bodies or boxes. It's also useful for decorative panels where you can take advantage of the grain to form beautiful patterns.

It's called bookmatching because you open up the halves of a resawn board like a book, so the grain patterns are symmetrical around the joint.

You can also bookmatch the successive slices of a matched log set, the set of boards formed by sequentially sawing a whole or quartered log; this is effectively resawing at full log scale. Contrast this with slip-matching, where you slip the sequenced workpieces side by side rather than flipping one over, which produces a repeating grain pattern sideways.

1

2

Start with a board that has been flattened on both faces and resawn. Unfold the halves on a long shooting board along the edge where you want to join them. Choose which edge to use based on the resulting grain pattern. The long shooting board is used for gang-planing the long-grain edge, so the stop on the end end does not have to be precisely at 90° like a shooting board made for shooting end grain. This provides precisely jointed edges that unfold and match up to a flat panel.

Fold the halves all the way back, so that the flat outer faces are back to back. This is like opening a book up and folding its covers all the way back so they meet. Set the paired halves on the shooting board so that the ends bump up against the stop and the the long grain overhangs the bed. You should have already planed the resawn faces mostly flat, so they sit flat and steady on the shooting board. Leave the last bit of planing for after the panel has been glued up.

3

4

Wax the side and bed of the plane with a block of beeswax, some paste wax or a candle.

Shoot the long grain of the halves together. Because the plane body is lying at 90° to the edge, this produces a perfectly square shot edge. But even if it isn't perfectly square, this will take advantage of complementary angles. When you unfold the workpieces and bring those edges together, they will form a perfectly matched joint.

5

Aim to finish the stroke past the end stop so that you get a smooth, consistent shot down the entire length, without rocking the plane. Long grain offers much less resistance than end grain, making this is easy to do down a long workpiece. Finish up with light, precise shavings.

6

Open the workpieces up and lay them on their flat outer faces. Match them up along the edge and inspect it. If there are any gaps visible, possibly the result of wobbling the plane during a stroke, fold them back and clean it up.

7

For final inspection, hold the matched workpieces up to the light and inspect all along the seam. No light should show through anywhere.

8

Glue-up is the same as a full-thickness panel. Spread a light bead of glue along both edges.

9

Tighten up the clamps carefully as you hold the joint down to prevent bowing or buckling. Look for a uniform squeeze-out along the entire length.

10

Put something on top to weigh it down while it dries. One issue when resawing wood is that you're exposing the wood inside the board to the air. Since it probably has a slightly different moisture content than the outer faces, it may cup a bit due to differential drying. You should stack and sticker freshly resawn wood for a day or two to equalize with the environment.

11

Scrape the glue once it has gotten rubbery, before it completely hardens. That reduces the chance of it tearing up the surface as the bits break off. On a thin panel, there's not a lot of margin for cleanup. Handle it carefully until the glue has cured completely, then flatten and smooth both sides with handplanes. One challenge in planing is that opening up the workpiece means that the two halves of the panel will have reversing grain at the joint. You'll need to plane each half in opposite directions. The scraper helps with the final surface along the joint, because it works with both grain directions.

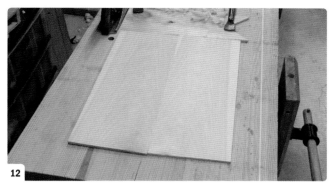

12

The finished panel has a tight joint and a symmetric visible pattern in the grain. Part of planning a bookmatch includes visualizing the final pattern so you can decide exactly where you want the joined edge. This can produce dramatic geometric patterns. For instance, I could have formed a spear-point triangular pattern in this grain by joining on a slight diagonal across the board rather than straight along its side.

COOPERED JOINTS

Coopered joints form a curved surface by edge-joining a series of segments on an angle. Then you'll plane and scrape the joints into the final curve.

This works for convex, concave and undulating curves.

1

Draw the curved surface full-size and divide it up into a series of segments. This will be the plan for shaping the angled edges of the flat segments that approximate the curve initially. Each joint bisects the angle of the curve at that point. Cut a series of workpieces wide enough for each of the segments.

2

Clamp a #7 jointer upside down in the vise. Instead of moving the jointer over the wood, you'll move the wood over the jointer. Be careful of the exposed blade. In particular, avoid running your fingers over it holding the wood.

3

Pitch the workpiece over at an angle and repeatedly pull it back over the iron to plane the edge at an angle.

4

Check the workpiece frequently against the plan and adjust the angle as necessary. Once you get a flat at the right angle, that will act as a reference surface for remaining passes. This is a very organic process, completely by eye.

5

You can also push the workpieces. Either way, you'll need to work both edges of each workpiece.

6

Stand up the workpieces and check each segment against the last one.

7

Join each new workpiece to the previous ones with a strip or two of blue tape on the outside. Lay everything edge-to-edge and stretch the tape tight across.

8

Form up the remaining segments. If a workpiece ends up too narrow, you can compensate by making the next workpiece a little wide. The final planing will round out the shape.

Orient all the workpieces so that you can plane the grain in the same direction on all the joints. Stretch two pieces of tape all the way across.

Spread glue in each of the individual joints just as for flat joints. For this simple shape, all I need is the clamps, and the segments will fall into the correct curve against the tape. For more complex shapes, make up a support form of shaped form workpieces and lay the segments in that. You may also need to do separate glue-ups for separate sections of the whole shape, then glue up these subassemblies.

Tighten the clamps carefully to make sure all the joints close up properly without pulling the tape loose.

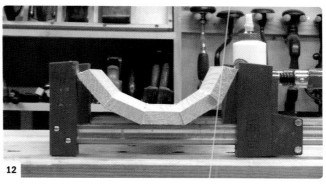

Check that the joints are all closed up at the end. Closed joints are the priority, even if that means the shape of the curve is slightly off. You'll clean that up in planing, as long as it's not too severe.

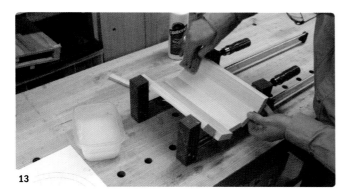

Clean up the glue on the inside of the curve before it hardens, since it will be harder to scrape on this curved surface.

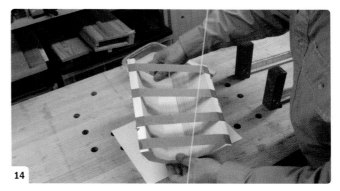

Another clamping strategy is to wrap tape or cord around the workpieces. This allows you to handle the assembly and helps distribute the clamping pressure across the joints. You can also wrap it around a form.

After the glue has dried, inspect the joints inside and out. Theses joints are good on the inside, but there are some definite gaps on the outside. That may indicate I tightened the clamps too much, closing up the inside well but opening up the outside.

Since this assembly is meant to be a convex surface, round out the joints with a spokeshave and block plane. You need to be creative figuring out how to secure a workpiece like this to the bench. For concave surfaces, round moulding planes or wide out-cannel gouges (gouges with the bevel on the outside) can hog out the waste, followed by curved scrapers to smooth out the curve.

Fair out the curve. This is where you can correct any minor deviations in the shape. The desired curve is in there under the excess wood, you just need to plane down to it. You can draw the curve profile on the end grain to help guide your planing. This also planes down past some of the gaps in the joint.

Use additional clamping setups as necessary to get good access to all the joints and support free-hanging sections. As usual, skewing the plane is the universal answer to helping with awkward sections.

After planing down, only one open gap remains. Fill gaps like these with a filler paste of glue and sawdust. At this point, the filler is just for appearance, it doesn't lend any strength to the joint. If you have a serious gap that risks joint failure, pare a long, thin wedge-shaped strip off the corner of a scrap to use as a filler strip. Glue this in along the entire gap to strengthen the joint.

Squirt some glue on a plastic lid, pile on some fine sawdust, and mix it together with a stick. If you plan to stain the workpiece, add a drop or two of stain to the mix to color the filler, because the dried glue will inhibit the stain later. It's worth doing a test batch and letting it dry to see how it comes out. If you can't get the desired color, you may want to use a commercial filler.

21

Press the filler into the gap to force it in. Gently wipe off any excess.

22

After the filler dries, plane or scrape it down smooth.

23

The final smooth, curved assembly, ready for trimming the ends. This assembly is quite strong – it held over 90 lbs in a test.

24

TONGUE & GROOVE JOINTS

The tongue-and-groove joint is an edge joint with a simple mechanical interlock. This is also known as "match planing," forming the matched halves of the joint.

The grooving operation cuts a groove of fixed width to a fixed depth, at a fixed distance from the edge. The tonguing operation cuts a matching tongue of the same fixed dimensions.

Grooving planes are also useful for cutting plain grooves if the fixed dimensions meet your needs.

Several different styles of match planes. They are made for specific sizes of tongue-and-groove on specific thicknesses of stock. You can use a specific set on a range of stock plus or minus up to 1/8" thickness. Left, a metal come-and-go plane with fixed fence. Center, a metal plane with rotating fence. Right, a pair of wooden moulding match planes.

(A) The grooving side of the metal come-and-go plane. The metal fence rides along the side of the workpiece while the iron plows out the groove. **(B)** The tonguing side. The metal fence rides along the side of the workpiece while the notched iron cuts down each side of the tongue.

(A) The grooving side of the rotating fence plane. The metal fence rides along the side of the workpiece while the single iron plows out the groove. **(B)** With the fence rotated around to the other position, the tonguing side. The metal fence rides along the side of the workpiece while the double irons cuts down each side of the tongue.

(A) The grooving plane of the matched set of wooden moulding planes. The metal skate rides in the groove cut by the narrow iron. **(B)** The matching tonguing plane. The groove in the plane rides on the tongue cut by the notched iron. Unfortunately, you often only find one of the pair at flea markets, because whoever sold them didn't realize they were a matched set.

A combination plane such as this Stanley #45 can also make tongue and groove joints. The iron must be changed out for each operation.

Using the Come-and-Go Plane

1

Forming the tongue with the come-and-go plane. It will bottom out once it has fully formed the tongue. With all of these planes, hold the fence snug up against the workpiece as you plane, and hold the plane up straight, square to the edge. If the plane is pitched over any, it won't form the joint properly.

2

Forming the matching groove. Just as with the tongue, the plane will bottom out when it has fully formed the groove. Make sure to register it against the proper face of the board so that the groove aligns with the tongue.

3

Fit the workpieces together and press into place. You can glue this up for a solid panel, but another use of this joint is to leave the workpieces floating to accommodate wood movement, for instance on the back of a casepiece. As they shrink apart forming a gap, the tongue keeps the gap from going all the way through.

4

The joint is snug and flush. It's offset from center in the edge because the plane is meant for $5/8$" stock, and this is ¾".

Using the Rotating Fence Plane

Forming the tongue with the rotating fence plane.

For the groove, pull the locking pin up and rotate the fence to the other position.

Forming the groove.

Fit the tongue and groove edges together.

Using the Wooden Plane

Forming the tongue with the wooden plane.

Forming the groove with the matching plane.

Fit the pieces together.

For a floating joint, you can chamfer or round the edge of each piece with a block plane. This creates a detail on the joint that's always there, so the gap doesn't look so obvious when it opens up. Celebrate the gap rather than hiding it.

The accentuated gap of the joint looks good both when tight and when open.

RABBETS

A step along a long-grain edge is a rabbet. Across end grain it's called a fillister. There are many ways to make rabbets and fillisters. The most basic methods use just chisels and saws, showing the versatility of these tools. Other methods use more specialized tools

A step along a long-grain edge is a rabbet. Across end grain it's called a fillister.

From left, chisels and joinery saws, wooden skew rabbet moulding plane, shoulder plane, metal rabbet plane, block skew rabbet plane, and moving fillister plane.

Rabbeting With a Chisel

1

To lay out for rabbetting with a chisel, mark the edge with a marking gauge for the depth of the rabbet.

2

Mark the adjoining face with the marking gauge for the width.

3

Start at the far end, bevel-down. Work right along the scribed width line.

4

Take scooping cuts to establish the initial step. Don't worry about the scalloped bottom, but concentrate on forming a clean shoulder line.

5

Work your way back along the edge. You can take big, deep chips as long as you don't go past your depth line. This will produce a very uneven surface that you'll clean up later. This is a roughing stage.

6

At the near end, come straight in. Start with a light cut until you see how the grain is reacting. Then you can go deeper for a more aggressive cut.

7 Make a second pass. Use the shoulder established by the first pass as a guide surface to register the side of the chisel.

8 Especially if you're working in hardwood with a long chisel, tuck it up into your shoulder and drive it with your upper body by leaning into it. Use your hand on the end to steer it. Another way to work on hardwood is to use continuous taps from a mallet. Either way, the bevel-down orientation gives you depth control, allowing you to lever out of a cut.

9 Take as many passes as you need to get close to the depth. Then clean up by laying the chisel down flat on its back, bevel-up, and pare across. Just be careful to avoid diving deep. This takes advantage of the long flat back, registering on the ledge of the rabbet. If the grain is cooperative, you can come in from the opposite direction as well.

10 To deal with problem spots, skew the chisel outward, as you slice down the length. Be careful not to dig the corner of the chisel into the wall of the rabbet.

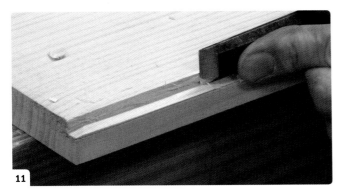

11 Clean up the wall the same way, paying attention to the grain. It's a combination of different motions along different dimensions in the best way that cooperates with the grain.

12 For final paring, use your fingers at the front as the main driver and control, with your hand at the back providing some extra power.

Drag the edge along the wall and floor of the rabbet to scrape it clean.

Making a Fillister With a Chisel

To make a fillister, mark the end grain for the depth, and across the grain for the width. The fillister presents a complication: You can't chisel across the solid grain the way you could down long grain. The solution is to saw across the grain. Run the marking knife along the scribe line to form a knifewall to guide the saw.

Set a crosscut joinery saw in the trough and carefully crosscut down just shy of the depth of the fillister. Don't go all the way, because that risks going too deep and leaving a saw line visible in the final joint.

This is the really fun part. Lay the chisel down flat, bevel-up, and roll up the cross grain. Don't take more than half the full depth. Then repeat with additional passes, taking half the remaining thickness, until you're just above the line. If your chisel is too short to go all the way across, skew it outward so the handle clears the work, or reverse the workpiece and come in from the other direction toward the middle.

Take the final careful parings right at the line, registering the flat back on the ledge. Since you didn't saw down exactly to this depth, that will raise some feathers along the edge. Some of these will break off easily when you brush off the shavings, although cutting them off in the next step leaves a cleaner wall.

5

Use your marking knife to cut off any remaining feathers and leave a crisp inside corner.

6

Drag the chisel back along the fillister to scrape it clean.

Ripsawing Rabbets

1

You can also make a rabbet entirely with a joinery ripsaw. Mark the depth and width with a marking gauge. Run the marking knife along the width line to form a knifewall.

2

Set the saw into the far end of the knifewall trough and start sawing lightly. Lower the saw and extend the length of the cut until the entire saw is working.

3

Keep working the saw back, until you've established a kerf along the entire length of the rabbet. Saw back and forth carefully until you just reach the full depth. Use the trigger finger grip to control the saw and keep it from wobbling, with light pressure from your other hand.

4

Run the marking knife along the depth line to form another knifewall.

5

Saw out along this trough the same way.

6

If necessary, saw down the last little bit in the first cut to free the waste.

The stick of waste will come free.

7

Sawing a Fillister

1

To make a fillister, use both crosscut and ripsaws. Mark the end grain and top grain with a gauge, and make the cross grain knifewall.

2

Crosscut down to just shy of the depth

3

Form the knifewall in the end grain.

4

With the ripsaw, saw down to width.

With the crosscut saw, carefully cut through the final fibers until the waste pops off.

5

Using an Antique Wooden Skew Rabbet Plane

1

The bottom of an antique wooden skew rabbet plane. The iron is skewed across. It's a rabbet plane because the iron comes all the way to the side, forming a corner that will plane out a rabbet. It also has a cutter on the side called a "nicker," used for cross grain to sever the fibers before the iron peels them up.

2

Since this plane has no fence or depth guide, you control it entirely by hand. Use your fingers as a fence on the bottom to control the width. You control depth by eye.

Hold the plane with your fingers bearing against the edge of the workpiece, positioning the corner of the iron at the width scribe line. Start at the far end with a short, light shaving and work your way back repeatedly, taking a series of short forward shavings along the entire length. Work carefully, because this establishes the edge of the rabbet and its initial shoulder.

The initial shoulder will serve as the reference for remaining passes.

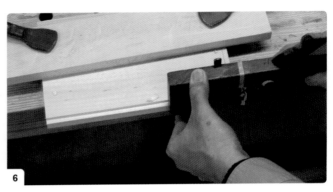

Holding the plane tight against that shoulder, take repeated full length passes, starting from the near end.

Now you can work more quickly. Hold the plane up straight, square to the board. Take it all the way down to the depth line, finishing with careful passes.

If the wall needs cleanup, lay the plane on its side from the other direction and plane down to the width line.

The completed rabbet.

Creating a Fillister With a Skew Rabbet Plane

1

2

For a fillister, tap the nicker down just past the bed of the plane so it will cut. This eliminates the need for a crosscut saw.

Set the nicker in the far end of the scribe line and draw it back to deepen the cut. Then push forward so the iron peels up a shaving. Work back repeatedly just as with the long-grain rabbet.

3

4

Once you have the initial shoulder established, take full-length passes, drawing the tool back so the nicker severs the fibers, then pushing forward to roll up the shaving. The nicker also cuts on the forward stroke.

The completed fillister.

Rabbeting With a Shoulder Plane

1

2

Use a shoulder plane similarly, with your fingers on the bottom acting as a fence. Like the rabbet plane, the iron comes all the way to the side of the plane. However, it's straight across, not skewed. A shoulder plane generally takes finer shavings than a wooden rabbet plane.

Start at the far end and take small cuts, working your way back. Pitch the nose of the plane down so that the precisely ground body of the plane registers in the shoulder you've already cut.

Once you have a full shoulder, take full-length passes, registering the plane against the deepening wall. Plane it all the way down to the line. If the wall needs cleanup, lay the plane down on its side and plane from the other direction.

The completed rabbet.

To make a fillister, first crosscut the end down near the depth. Then plane across. This is similar to using a chisel, except that you have the body of the plane registering to control the cut.

The completed fillister.

Using an Antique Metal Rabbet Plane

Antique metal rabbet plane, with a bullnose position at the front. The bullnose allows you to make a rabbet up close into a corner.

A common problem with these is that they're missing the fence and depth stop. It does have its nicker.

You can clamp a guide with jointed edge along the width line to act as a fence. This works with wooden skew rabbet and shoulder planes as well.

The completed rabbet and fillister.

Use the nicker guided along the fence to make a fillister.

Rabbeting With a Skew Block Plane

The skew block plane is perfect for rabbeting. It does have a fence, but it's made to have a wooden guide attached to it, so the fence doesn't come over far enough for a small rabbet.

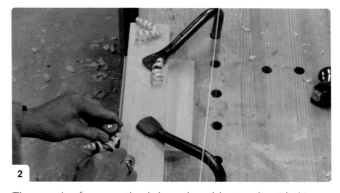

The wooden fence method along the rabbet works with this. This plane produces beautiful fine ribbon shavings.

3

This plane does an excellent job making a fillister, using the nicker.

4

The completed rabbet and fillister.

Rabbeting With a Moving Fillister Plane

1

The final tool we'll examine is the moving fillister plane. The moving part of it is the fence on the bottom that sets the width of the cut.

2

It also has a depth stop, as well as a nicker.

3

You don't need to mark the width or depth on the workpiece. Set the fence and depth stop on the plane. Hold the fence up against the edge and take full length passes. Keep going until the brass foot bottoms out along the entire length. Be sure to hold the plane straight up and square to the work.

4

To make a fillister, use the fence and depth stop the same way, and use the nicker the same as on the wooden rabbet plane. Draw it back to score the surface, then plane forward.

The completed rabbet and fillister.

Additional Rabbeting Tips

If the grain is going the wrong direction to plane it flat on the bench, mount the workpiece edge up in the vise. This orients the grain properly. It also switches the width and depth of the rabbet, so be sure to adjust the settings appropriately.

Plane along the edge.

When you rabbet at a corner with a plane, the front of the plane will prevent you from getting all the way into the corner, even with a bullnose rabbet plane. Get as close into the corner as you can, then finish it either with a chisel, or with a chisel plane. This shoulder plane has a removable nose that converts it into a chisel plane.

You can also use a plow plane with a wide iron to form a rabbet, since a rabbet is just an open-sided groove. This offers the fence and depth control of the moving fillister plane.

GROOVES

Grooves are long-grain excavations in edges and faces. Think of them as a three-sided trench that runs with the grain.

The grooving planes for tongue-and-groove joints can be used to make other grooves. The limitation is that they make a specific groove of a fixed width at a fixed position. If there's a particular groove you make frequently, you can make a simple dedicated grooving plane for it.

Like rabbets, the most basic methods of cutting grooves use chisels and saws. Other methods use more specialized tools such as shoulder planes and plow or combination planes.

When you use chisels for grooving, you can use router planes to clean up the bottoms and ensure they are at a consistent depth. These are also useful for similar cleanup of rabbets and other joints.

A plow plane has a fence to set its position from the edge of the workpiece. The simplest style of plow plane is the wooden wedge-arm plow, where wedges lock the fence into place.

The width of the groove is determined by the width of the plane iron. Different manufacturers had different numbering systems. A common problem is that people don't realize there's a whole set of cutters that goes along with these planes, so when you find them, most of the time you just get whatever iron happens to be in the plane at the time. The other irons are lost somewhere in the mists of time. When you buy replacement irons, make sure they fit in the mortise at the top of the plane.

To loosen the wedge and iron, tap sharply on the back of the plane with a mallet. Also, notice that for any plane with a tapered iron, the wedge and iron form opposing wedges, so you can also tap down sharply on the top of the iron to drive it through until loose.

The different irons neck down to the specific groove width. The iron has a groove in the back that aligns to the metal skate. That supports it and keeps it from rocking side to side. To set an iron, slide it into the mortise and fit the groove onto the skate, then wedge it tight. The amount that the iron protrudes past the skate determines the thickness of the shaving. To advance the iron, tap it forward and tap the wedge to tighten it up. To retract it, tap on the back of the plane, then tap the wedge to tighten it up.

Turn the brass knob on the top to set the depth stop foot.

This screw arm plow works the same as the wedge arm plow, except that you turn these wooden nuts to adjust the fence position and lock it down.

The Stanley #45 combination plane makes an excellent plow. It has a number of irons that allow it to be used for mouldings and match joints as well. The idea is that this single plane can replace an entire chest of wooden moulding planes. However, they've garnered mixed reviews over the years. They can be finicky to set up, and each time you switch irons, you have to set them up again. Dedicated moulding planes allow you to switch back and forth between profiles with no further setup.

(A) This knob advances and retracts the iron. (B) In addition to the fence and depth stop adjustments of the wooden plow planes, the #45 has an adjustable skate that you set to the width of the iron.

Grooving With a Chisel

To make a groove with a chisel, set the points of a mortise gauge's pins to the exact width of the chisel. Set the gauge fence to position the groove the desired distance from the workpiece edge.

Hold the fence of the gauge tight against the reference face of the workpiece and run it down the edge to mark the position and score the surface fibers.

If you don't have a dual-pin marking gauge, you can mark with a single-pin or cutting gauge. You can mark both lines from the reference face, setting it to the distance for each one. Alternatively, you can set it for one distance, then mark that same distance from both faces. This perfectly centers the groove.

The rest of the process is like rabbeting with a chisel. Start at the far end, bevel-down, and carefully pare out chips to establish the initial depth.

5

With the initial cut established, take repeated passes to deepen it. You can use your fingers as a makeshift plane body to hold the chisel steady and run it along the groove. Take scooping cuts on difficult spots. Finish up with a light continuous pass.

6

To get a smooth, uniform depth, use a small router plane after roughing out the groove with the chisel. Set it for a light cut. Some routers also have a fence on the bottom to help with grooving. Start at the far end and work back, then finish up with a continuous full-length pass. You can push or pull the router, as long as you go with the grain.

7

If you have some high spots, tip the router up to raise the cutting edge and take a lighter cut. Work the spot down until you can pass smoothly over it. Once the router bottoms out for the entire length, you've reached full depth.

8

A variation of the basic chisel method is to saw down the walls of the groove with a joinery ripsaw. Start the cut at the far end after marking the lines.

9

Extend the cut until you can saw full-length along the edge. Repeat for the second wall.

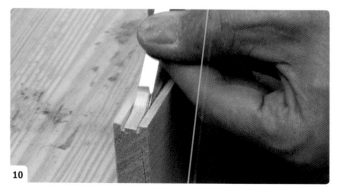

10

Chisel out the waste between the saw kerfs.

11

12

Sawing out the walls allows you to take heavier cuts with the chisel. Finish the groove the same as the plain chisel method.

The finished groove.

Grooving a Face

1

2

Grooving a face is exactly the same. For wider grooves or harder woods, use a mallet to drive the chisel. It provides short impulses of force to cut in. Use the chisel bevel-down for depth control.

Finish with a large router. Wax the bottom to lubricate it. You can use it pushing or pulling. Rather than moving it with both handles at once, hold one handle in place and pivot the router on that point, using the leverage provided by the other handle. This allows it to take a heavier cut. Then finish up with light full-length passes.

3

4

For high spots, pitch the router up on its front edge and use the pivoting action to nibble through. Lower the router back down as it clears the spot.

The router isn't suitable for heavy stock removal. Use the coarse, medium, and fine strategy. Do the heavy, coarse work with a chisel. Do the medium work with the router, set for a heavy cut. Do the final, fine work with it set for a light cut, removing just a thin layer.

5

The finished groove.

6

If your shoulder plane fits in the groove, it does nicely here, either freehand or against a fence. You can do the entire groove with the shoulder plane, or use it as a finishing tool after roughing with a chisel. If the grain is going the wrong way, you can pull it.

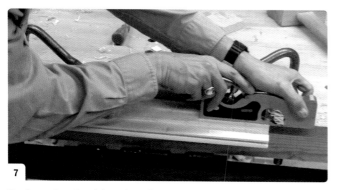

7

Pushing the shoulder plane from the other side.

8

The finished groove. You can also run the shoulder plane between saw kerfs.

Grooving With a Plow Plane

1

Plow planes are the real champions here, because this is what they were made for. Work from the end back until you have an initial groove established, then take full-length passes.

2

Be sure to hold it straight up, not tipped, with the fence pressed tight against the work. Plows work best taking light shavings. But even then they make quick work.

The plow plane works the same way on the face.

Grooving With a Stanley #45

The Stanley #45 does an excellent job grooving. Use it the same as a wooden plow. There are also simpler dedicated metal plow planes.

It quickly produces a cloud of ribboned shavings to form the groove.

To make a groove wider than your available irons, make a first groove at one side, then adjust the fence to widen it and make a second groove at the other side.

DADOS

Dados are cross-grain grooves. The cross-grain orientation limits your choices. You don't have the variety of methods available for the previous joints.

After the methods for rabbets and grooves, this technique will be very familiar. It's a combination of using crosscut joinery saw, chisel and router plane. The marking knife and square are critical for layout, and bench hooks hold the workpiece.

To make a dado to fit another component into, butt the square tight up to the reference edge and strike a line along it with a marking knife for the first side. Place the square so that you're marking on the waste side of the line. That way, any angling of the knife or stray marks will be in the waste, leaving a crisp edge on the good side. Don't knife the other side of the dado.

Run the knife down the waste side of the line to form a knifewall trough.

Set the workpiece that will fit in the dado against the knife line and draw a light pencil line along the other side. Make a tick mark down over the edges as well. This is just an approximate position, to highlight the waste area so you don't accidentally work on the wrong side of the line.

Set a router plane to the depth of the dado. Use it as a gauge to mark the depth at both ends of the joint, along both edges, unless the dado will be stopped before an edge.

6 A

6 B

(A) Marking the depth on an edge. **(B)** The marked end of the joint.

7

8

Set a crosscut joinery saw into the trough and carefully saw down to the marked depth. Run the saw against your fingertips to keep it from jumping out of the cut and marking the wood. For a stopped dado, angle the saw up slightly to deepen the cut at the end. Then angle it down and use the tip to cut near the stop position. Lower the saw and saw flat across to depth within that stopped kerf.

Secure the workpiece to the workbench. Using a chisel free-hand or with a mallet, bevel-up or bevel-down, chisel down in the waste up to the knife line, forming an initial shoulder.

9

10

Make an additional pass to deepen the shoulder, cutting from about the center of the dado. Run the marking knife along this shoulder if necessary to clear any chips.

This is the critical step to a good fit. Stand the other workpiece against the shoulder, tipped over the ridge of waste in the dado. Hold it firm against the shoulder.

11

With the tip of the marking knife, make a tick mark to show the width of the workpiece. This will be the width of the dado. This is where things can go wrong. If the knife is tipped out away from the workpiece, the tip may be undercutting the width. If it's tipped too close, it may mark too wide. It's worth making some practice dados to get the proper balance. If the dado ends up too tight, you can widen it slightly, but you can't tighten one that's too loose.

12

Turn the workpiece around and butt the square against the reference edge. Set the tip of the knife in the tick mark and slide the square over to it. The square is now positioned and oriented to allow you to mark the second wall of the dado in the waste. Strike the knife line.

12

Form the trough for this knifewall.

14

Saw down this wall the same as the first one.

15

Secure the workpiece to the bench and chisel out this side. Since it's already been chiseled on the other side of the ridge, this is easier.

16

This leaves a triangular ridge down the center of the dado. Use a chisel narrower than the dado to remove the ridge.

17

Place the edge of the chisel in the depth line you marked with the router. Angle the handle down and bump the handle to pop a chip off the end. This prevents blowing out the edge when chiseling in from the other direction.

18

Turn the workpiece around and repeat on the other end.

19

Raise the handle and chisel straight across, rolling up the ridge. Don't go all the way to full depth; leave a shaving or two.

20

If the chisel is long enough, go all the way to the far end. Since you popped out the chip, there's no danger of blowing out fibers. Otherwise, turn the workpiece around and chisel in from that side.

21 A

21 B

The best way to finish the dado to final depth is with a router plane **(A)**, because it's guaranteed to get it to a consistent depth. Work in from both sides to the middle. Depending on the grain, you may find it easier to work from one side versus the other. The second choice is to use a shoulder plane **(B)** that's narrower than the dado. It doesn't have a guide to show depth, so you have to watch as you plane down to the marks at each end. Make sure the plane is running flat so there are no bumps or dips in the middle.

22

Fit the workpiece into the dado. The fit should be snug enough that you need a little hand pressure to seat it, but not so tight that you have to hammer it in place. Soft wood will compress to fit in a tight joint, but hard wood won't, so it risks damaging something.

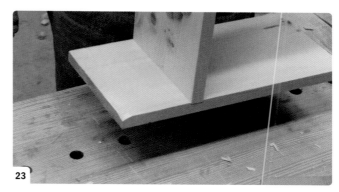

23

You should be able to lift the assembly without the joint falling apart.

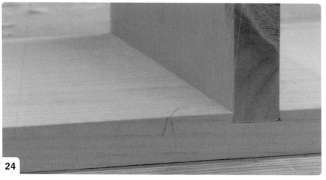

24

The final dado should bottom out snugly at each end, and run back to the far side with a smooth crisp shoulder on both sides. Small gaps in the end can be filled with glue and sawdust or commercial filler.

25

If the dado is too tight, a side rabbet plane is a specialized tool to widen it. This one is a single tool with two irons, one in each direction. There are also versions that are two separate planes.

26

Pick which wall to adjust and plane from both ends into the middle. That's why it has two irons. They need to be extremely sharp to take clean shavings and avoid chipping out the shoulder.

27

The plane takes tiny little shavings. Check the fit frequently. It's easy to overdo the adjustment and make it too loose. If you don't have a side rabbet plane, you can scribe a new knife line along the wall and chisel straight down, one chisel width at a time.

An Alternative Method

An alternative method to sawing the walls is to chop straight down with a chisel all along the length.

Alternate chopping down with chiseling out chips until you are at the full depth. All the other steps are the same. A third method uses dedicated dado planes, such as wooden planes similar to the wooden skew rabbet plane. They have an additional iron at the front that has nickers on both sides. There are also metal dado planes similar to the metal tongue and groove plane. Dedicated planes make dados of specific widths.

Both the saw method and the chisel method can make dados of any width. They can also make angled dados, such as the tapered dado in this shooting board for the wedged stop.

HALF-LAP JOINTS

There are many types of half-lap joints, also called "halving joints." Laps can be other proportions besides half thickness, such as one-third. The process for any proportion is the same except for the different thickness of the layout.

Precise sawing is critical to the success of these joints and those that follow. Joint lines will be highly visible, especially the shoulder lines. All the crosscuts need to be first-class cuts, for appearance and fit.

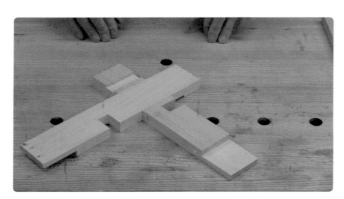

Half-lap cross, made in the faces.

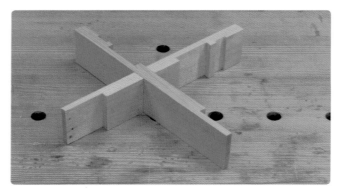

Notched half-lap, which is a half-lap made in the edge.

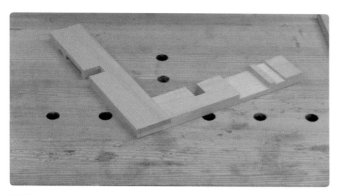

Half-lap corner, made in the ends.

Since lap joints are like short, wide dados, the tools are the same, except for the addition of a rip joinery saw for half-lap corners.

Consistent stock preparation is also important, since parts need to match in thickness or width to get flat joints. For notched lap joints, pair up the workpieces and gang-plane them to final width.

Making a Half-Lap Joint in Faces

1

To make a half-lap joint in the faces, lay the parts together at the proper position and draw light pencil lines on each side. Flip them over and do the same on the other face. These are not precise lines, they just show approximate position to keep everything oriented properly.

2

Butt the square against the reference edge of the workpiece at the position of the first shoulder and knife a line along it.

Run the knife along the waste side of the line to form a knifewall.

Use the center-finding technique for setting the marking gauge, and mark a center line along each edge between the shoulder positions. Run a pencil down these lines to make them more visible.

Set the router plane to this depth for later. The edge of the iron should fit exactly in the line.

Set the crosscut joinery saw in the knifewall trough and saw to the depth mark, running the saw against your fingertips so it doesn't jump out of the cut.

Secure the workpiece to the bench and chisel down the waste along the cut, taking a couple of passes to form the shoulder.

Hold the edge of the other workpiece firmly against the shoulder and make a tick mark at the position of the second shoulder.

9

Spin the workpiece around, set the knife point into the tick mark, butt the square against the reference edge, and slide it over to the knife. That puts the square exactly in position. Knife the second shoulder line along the square.

10

Run the knife down in the waste to form the knifewall.

11

Crosscut this shoulder like the first one. Then make additional crosscuts spaced less than your chisel width to divide the waste into segments.

12

Secure the workpiece to the bench and use the chisel angled up to pop off the waste at the edge, bumping the end of the handle with your palm or a mallet. Don't do it full depth, start halfway so you can see what the grain is going to do and avoid nasty surprises. Here I've put a scrap behind the workpiece as a spacer to move it closer to the edge of the bench.

13

Take additional cuts along the edge, dividing the remaining depth in half each time until you get right down to the line.

14

Turn the workpiece around and repeat this process to bump off the other edge and take it down to the line.

15

Roll up all the waste in the hump in the middle, using hand pressure or a mallet. Keep the chisel pointed slightly upward so it doesn't dive down into the grain, and rough it out in several passes.

16

Do a final light chisel pass just above full depth.

17

Using the router that you previously set for the proper depth, do the final fine cleanup. Work in from both sides to the middle, spinning the workpiece around to butt it up against the bench hooks. Be sure to clean out the corners of the shoulders.

18

The finished workpiece after scraping out any stray fibers with the chisel.

19

The process is exactly the same for the mating workpiece, again working from the reference edge.

20

The one difference is that when you chisel out the first shoulder and set the first workpiece into it to find the location of the second shoulder, the lap that you cut into the first workpiece drops down into place here. Hold it snugly in place as you make the tick mark with the knife.

21

After completing the remaining steps on the second piece, fit the two together. Like the dado, a good fit means you need some hand pressure to press the joint home, but you don't need to hammer it in place. The joint should stay together when you lift it.

22

A common problem is that the joint isn't quite flush. That means the cuts are just shy of half thickness. This is easy to correct.

23

Adjust the router to take a thin additional shaving. Route this shaving from inside each lap.

24

Now the joint closes up flush, on both front and back sides. If the joint is flush just on one side, that means the workpieces aren't equal thickness. Plane the thick one down carefully, one shaving at a time until it's flush.

An alternative to finishing with the router plane is to pare the last few shavings with a paring chisel sharpened at a low angle. Use your thumb to hold the chisel down flat and drive it. Move the end in circular, shearing motions slightly skewed to the cut, to delicately slice down the high spots. Skewing and slicing gives you very fine control and leaves a good surface. The flat back of the chisel bears against the face as a reference surface to keep it from diving in.

25

Making a Notched Joint

1

Start a notched joint by marking the approximate width of each workpiece on the other in pencil.

2

With the square butted against the reference face, knife the line for the first shoulder.

3

Draw the approximate lines halfway down the faces.

4

Use the center-finding method to set the marking gauge to the center of the workpiece, and mark across between the pencil lines front and back. Run a pencil along the line to make it more visible.

5

Bring the top knife line down the sides. Set the tip of the knife edge in the line, slide the square over to it, then then run the knife down the square to the gauged line at the halfway point.

6

Secure the piece workedge-up in the vise, high enough to clear the guage line.

With a chisel, remove a small chip along the knife line. This forms the knifewall.

Set the crosscut joinery saw in the knifewall trough and saw down to the gauge line.

With the chisel, take a larger chip to form a shoulder.

Hold the matching workpiece snugly against the shoulder so you can mark the width of the notch.

Make a tick mark with the knife point at the position of the second shoulder.

Set the knife point in the mark, butt the square against the reference face, and slide it over to the knife. Scribe the second shoulder line.

13

Bring this line down the sides to the gauge line.

14

Remove a chip to form the knifewall.

15

Saw down the second shoulder.

16

Using a chisel just narrower than the notch, chop down to remove half the waste. Check the other side to see what the grain is doing.

17

If the grain caused the chisel to undercut like this, remove the remaining waste from this side. Chop repeatedly to remove half the remaining waste each time, stopping just shy of the gauge line.

18

Pare the final shavings at the gauge lines from each side with the chisel tipped slightly to leave a hump in the middle. Then pare that hump down flat to the lines.

19

Repeat these steps for the mating workpiece, then fit them together. Once again, the joint should need some hand pressure to go together, and should hold together when you lift up.

20

The joint doesn't quite meet flush.

21

Hold a block against the lower workpiece as you hit it with a mallet to separate the joint.

22

Pare a shaving from each joint, then fit them back together. Repeat as necessary until they fit flush.

23

The final joint is flush top and bottom.

24

This process works for other angles as well, both on faces and edges. The only difference is in scribing the lines at some angle. All the other steps of sawing, chiseling and finishing with router plane are the same.

Corner Half-Lap Joints

1

2

The half-lap joint at a corner increases the challenge, because in addition to the shoulder lines, the ends of the workpieces will be visible. Start by marking the approximate width of each piece on the other. Provide a little extra width so that each end will be proud of the other. You'll plane these flush after gluing.

On the first workpiece, scribe a knife line along the square.

3

4

Form the knifewall.

Set the marking gauge for half the thickness, and mark that along the edges and across the end grain. Run a pencil down the line for visibility.

5

6

Crosscut the shoulder line down to the gauge line.

Secure the workpiece in the vise with a corner up. Using a rip joinery saw, start sawing down the corner a couple shavings from the gauge line. This is the cheek cut.

7

Saw diagonally across the corner until you reach the shoulder cut along the side. It should be past the halfway point on the end grain.

8

Flip the workpiece over and saw the other corner diagonally down to the shoulder line.

9

Stand the workpiece up and saw down flat to the shoulder line. The diagonal kerfs help guide the saw the rest of the way. Remove the scrap of cheek waste. You might have to snap it off the last little bit.

10

Repeat these steps on the other piece. Take them down to the line with the router plane.

11

Since the cheek is open on one end, use the mating piece butted up against it to support the router on both sides, visible here on the right side of the photo. Route from both edges to the middle, and do it in a couple of passes, taking light shavings. Repeat on the mating joint.

12

Check the fit. Like the other joints, it's not quite flush. Take an additional shaving off each workpiece until the joint lies perfectly flush.

13

Notice how each end overhangs the other. This is the bit of extra width that needs to be planed flush after gluing.

14

Glue up the joint. Clean off the excess once it's gotten rubbery.

15

After the glue has dried, plane off the excess end grain with a block plane, skewed to the cut.

16

Do the final flush up with a fine-set smoother.

The final joint flush on shoulders and edges.

17

Alternatives

You can use a shoulder plane as an alternative to the router for final cleanup. Doubling up the two workpieces provides a long, flat surface to support the plane through the entire cut and keep it from drooping over one edge or the other. Since there's no depth control, you have to watch carefully to get a consistent flat surface over the entire faces and avoid going too far.

The most basic method is to pare across with a chisel. Use the back of the chisel on the flat registration surface for consistency. This method requires the most manual control.

CHAPTER 5
MORTISE & TENON JOINERY

MORTISE & TENON FIST FIGHTS & FUNDAMENTALS

There are two main arguments about making the mortise-and-tenon joint.

Mortises

The first argument concerns making mortises. Should you chop out your mortise waste with a chisel, or drill it out and then pare it with a chisel?

Chopping

1

Chopping with a chisel means chopping down across the grain.

2

Make a series of repeated chops to rough out the waste and finish the mortise.

Drilling

1

Drilling and paring the waste means boring a series of holes with a drill, and then paring to the line with a chisel.

2

Drill a series of holes to rough out the waste.

3

Finish up with a chisel.

4

Pare to the line for exact width.

Both methods work well. The chopping method does the entire job all at once. The drilling method splits it into rough and fine stages.

The chopping method is simpler because it requires fewer tools. The width of the mortise is determined by the width of the chisel you use.

There are two nice things about the drilling method. First, pounding on a chisel with a mallet is the noisiest thing you can

do with hand tools. If you're in a location where you need to be quiet – for instance a second floor apartment with neighbors underneath, or in the basement under your kid's bedroom – the drilling method is a much quieter style of woodworking.

Second, if you have large mortises, or odd sizes larger than your chisels, you can drill them out with any number of holes to rough out the required length and width. In thick, heavy wood, this can be a lot of work with a chisel.

Tenons

Sawing a tenon cheek.

Sawing right to the line, so that you can fit the tenon directly off the saw, requires fewer steps, but it is a more challenging cut in order to get a perfectly flat face.

Sawing away from the line is a rough operation that doesn't require precision.

Then paring right to the line is a fine operation. Even if you saw to the line, an extra paring step allows you to clean up sawing imperfections.

There are many variations of this joint. The hole is the mortise, and the tongue that fits in it is the tenon. This is a haunched tenon, where the notched haunch of the tenon fits in the groove of the mortised piece.

This is also an example of a blind mortise-and-tenon joint, where the tenon doesn't go all the way through. Nothing is visible on the outside.

A mortise and wedged through tenon. Through joints are more complicated because the end of the joint is visible, along with any imperfections in the fit. The wedge adds strength to lock the joint in place as it spreads the split tenon. Whatever the orientation of the tenon to the mortised piece, the wedge must be oriented at 90° to the grain of the mortised piece. If it was aligned with that grain, it would split the piece when it was driven in. The end grain faces of the mortise can also be angled out so that the split tenon forms a dovetail. Wedging round tenons is a common way of joining chair legs to seats, to keep the legs from coming loose.

Whatever the style of mortise-and-tenon, there should be a nice snug fit between the tenon and the matching mortise. It should require a little bit of hand pressure to slip them together. If you need to hammer it together, it's too tight, risking splitting. If the piece slips in with no resistance and won't hold together on its own, it's too loose.

The joint should have a clean, flat shoulder line, mating up precisely. It takes repeated practice to get consistent joints that fit well. Make one, cut it off, make another and repeat.

The width of the mortise, which is the thickness of the matching tenon, should be between one third and one half the thickness of the workpiece. If it's wider than one half the thickness, you'll end up with very thin walls that will break out easily. If it's narrower than one third, you'll end up with a very thin tenon, which will snap off easily. It's a balance between those in order to have thick enough walls and a thick enough tenon.

The other determining factor is the width of your tools, whether you're using mortising chisel, bench chisel or drill bit. Pick a tool that fits within that one third to one half range for excavating the mortise, and that will determine the thickness of the matching tenon. That's a good reason to do the mortise first. Then make the tenon to fit.

The mortise piece has about a ½" of extra length on the end. This is called the "horn." This reinforces the end while you work on the joint so the chisel doesn't split it out.

To trim the horn once you've glued up the joint and the glue has dried, crosscut it off about 1/16" away from the line.

Mount the joint in the vise with the horn end grain up, so that you can plane from the outside edge to the middle.

Carefully plane across with a sharp, fine-set smoother or block plane. Skew the plane to the cut to leave a clean surface. Register the front of the plane bed against the edge of the rail as you flush the end of the stile down to it.

The end of the stile flush with the edge of the rail. The shoulder line is also flush, as well as the end of this through tenon.

The second argument concerns making tenons. Should you fit them directly off the saw, or should you pare them to fit?

BLIND MORTISE & TENON

In frame-and-panel construction utilizing mortise-and-tenon joints, the cross piece is called a rail, like the rail of a fence. The upright is called a stile. Mortises are typically made in the stiles, and tenons are typically made in the rails, though some projects may call for different orientation.

The faces and edge of each piece must be square all around, with a reference face and edge marked on each one. The ends don't need to be perfectly squared up, because the stile ends have the extra length for the horns at each mortise, and the tenoned rail ends will be buried in the mortises.

The tools for making mortise-and-tenon joints vary depending on which method you'll use for clearing the mortises. The basic tools are tenon saws in crosscut and rip configuration, marking gauge with mortising pins, a narrow chisel that you'll use for clearing out the mortise, marking knife, small ruler and square.

To clear the mortise by chopping with a chisel, you need a bench chisel, a sash mortise chisel or an oval bolstered mortise chisel of the proper width. The width of the chisel determines the width of the mortise, and therefore the thickness of the tenon.

To use the drill-and-pare method to clear the mortise, you need a brace and bit and either a wide bench chisel or a wide paring chisel. The size of the bit determines the width of the mortise. The paring chisel can also be used for paring the tenon cheeks. The wider, the better.

1

The minimalist method is to chop the mortise with a chisel, and fit the tenon right off the saw. Mark some extra length on the end of the stile for the horn. Set the rail on the stile's reference edge and mark the approximate position of its width on it.

2

Measure ⅛" to ¼" in from each mark. That will determine the length of the mortise.

3

Square those lines across. These are the mortise end marks.

4

On the end of the rail, mark the length of the tenon. This one is 1½".

5

Set the pins of the marking gauge to the width of the chisel, and set the fence of the gauge so it will center the mortise in the stile.

6

Butt the marking gauge against the reference face and roll the points into each mortise end mark to dimple it. Pull or push the gauge from one end of the mortise to the other, until it clicks into the dimples and stops. Darken the line scribe lines with a pencil. These are the mortise width marks. Mark X's in the waste.

7

The marked-out mortise.

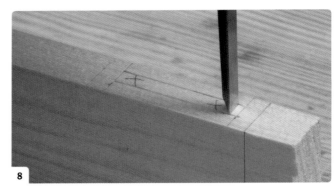

8

Set the chisel about ⅛" away from the end mark, with the bevel pointing in the direction of travel, toward the far end. Starting away from the end prevents damaging it while you work. You'll advance the chisel in a succession of chops. With each strike of the mallet, the wedging action of the bevel will push the chisel back into the already-chopped portion, clearing the waste. Each chop will go deeper than the last.

9

Take a single light tap with the mallet for the first chop, just enough to break the surface, then advance the chisel by about ⅛".

10

Take a single heavier tap to chop more deeply. The first chop acted as a relief cut, so this one starts to break out a chip.

11

Advance the chisel another ⅛". Now you can start to be more aggressive with the mallet, taking two or more heavy strikes for each chop. Continue advancing in this fashion, going deeper and deeper each time. Whenever you remove the chisel, tip it forward to lever out the waste behind it. Work it forward and back to sweep the walls of the mortise clear. Just be careful not to bury the chisel so deep that you risk snapping it as you lever, especially when using a bench chisel. You can be more aggressive with a heavy mortising chisel.

12

Hold the chisel up straight in the width of the mortise. The most important things are to keep it from twisting as it drives in, and not to pitch it to one side or the other. Either of these will result in denting or widening the walls of the mortise. You can pitch the chisel forward or back along the length of the mortise to help it cut.

13

Take the final chop about ⅛" from the second end. Just like the first end, this preserves the ends of the mortise while you work. You'll chop out that last bit of end waste as the final step.

14

Use a narrow chisel to clear out the waste. The progressive chopping has created a slope inside the mortise. Run the chisel down this to release chips and dig them out. The narrow width keeps this chisel from jamming up in the mortise.

15

Reverse the chisel so the bevel is pointing toward the first end, start at the second end and repeat the series of chops. Since this produces progressively deeper cuts eating up the slope formed by the first cut, the net result is a roughly level bottom on the mortise.

16

At the end, tip the chisel back so that the bevel rides flat down the surface as you chop. Clean out the waste with the narrow chisel.

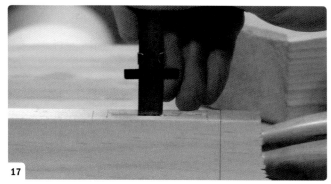

17

Check the depth. The mortise should be about ⅛" deeper than the length of the tenon. That allows room for glue to pool in the bottom as you glue it up. Otherwise the hydraulic effect of the glue prevents the joint from going together. Repeat the cycle of chopping as many times as necessary to get to the desired depth. This is a 2"-wide piece, and the tenon will be 1½", so the mortise needs to be at least 1⅝" deep.

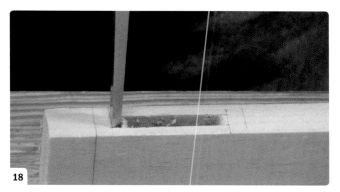

18

Set the chisel directly on the end mark, with the bevel facing into the mortise. Chop straight down to remove the end waste. Because there's nothing supporting the waste, it should be an easy chop.

19

Repeat on the other end.

20

If the bottom needs some cleanup, use the tip of the narrow chisel to poke straight down to break up any high spots, then scrape across. Be careful to keep the chisel away from the sides and ends so you don't damage them. The bottom doesn't need to be perfectly flat. It just needs to be deep enough to seat the tenon completely and allow room for glue squeeze-out.

Making the Matching Tenon

1

Make a mark 1½" from the end of the rail for the length of the tenon.

2

Set the knife point at the mark, butt the square against the reference edge of the rail, slide the square over to the knife and scribe a line across. This will be the shoulder line.

3

Scribe the line all around, butting the square against the reference face or reference for each side. Always set the end of the knife in the previous line and slide the square up to it.

4

Butt the gauge against the reference face and roll the points into the scribe line on the edge to lightly dimple it.

5 Pull the gauge from the end until the pins click into the dimples, then repeat on the other side. Run the gauge across the end grain, coming from both sides to the middle. Run a pencil down the gauge lines for visibility.

6 Because the shoulder cuts are first-class cuts, run a knifewall all around the shoulder lines.

7 Set the crosscut saw against the crisp shoulder edge established by the knifewall. Put your thumb against the saw to keep it from jumping back on the good wood and crosscut down to the gauge lines.

8 Flip the piece over and repeat on the second shoulder. Watch the far side of the cut carefully to avoid going past the line.

9 For the cheek cuts with the ripsaw, mount the piece in the vise with a corner up.

10 This requires very precise sawing, exactly on the waste side of the line. To guide the saw, use the marking knife to cut down across the corner, right on the line.

11

Make a second cut coming into that cut from the waste to form a notch. Repeat on the other side of the tenon.

12

A notched corner is the equivalent of making a knifewall for a crosscut. When you set the saw into it, the side of the saw is positioned in the waste right up against the the line.

13

Pinch your fingers on the corner as a guide to keep the saw from jumping out, and saw diagonally across the first corner.

14

Hold the saw with a relatively loose, relaxed grip – don't overgrip it. Too tight a grip tends to reduce your control. Watch carefully that each saw stroke continues right along the line, on both the edge grain and the end grain. Saw smoothly for the full length of the saw. Raise and lower the angle of the saw to extend the cut in each dimension. Cut as far as the shoulder line on the edge, and at least halfway across on the end.

15

Repeat the cut on the other corner.

16

Flip the piece over in the vise and notch the remaining corners.

17 Saw these corners, connecting the cuts on the end grain. This forms a triangle of uncut material on each cheek.

18 Stand the piece upright in the vise and saw straight down. The existing kerfs help guide the saw. You don't need a lot of pressure. Put your hand on top to help steady it, and keep a loose grip.

19 Support the scrap on the side with your fingers to keep it from snapping off prematurely while sawing.

20 Repeat on the second cheek.

21 Inspect each side to see that it's generally flat. There will be saw marks, but ideally no major bumps or irregularities. There is often some short grain in the shoulder where the cheek scrap came off.

22 Use a wide chisel to clean up the shoulder. Run the marking knife along the inside corner to remove any stray fibers, or chop down with hand pressure using the chisel.

23

The shoulder plane is an excellent tool for cleaning up defects. Different models have different adjustments. On this one, you can loosen the top screw, then adjust the front the screw to open or close the mouth. Use it with a tight mouth, so that you're removing very small amounts. Be sure to keep it flat as you go across, so it doesn't droop and end up planing a hump in the middle.

24

The most obvious use for a shoulder plane is to plane the shoulders, across the shoulder end grain. This allows you to fine-tune the fit of the rail to the stile. To avoid breaking out the grain on the far corner, plane from both corners into the middle.

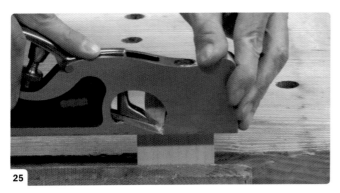

25

Plane in the other direction from the other corner.

26

Another strategy is to put a scrap on the edge to back it up as you plane across.

27

You can plane both shoulders this way, or spin the piece around, backing up the other edge, to do the second shoulder.

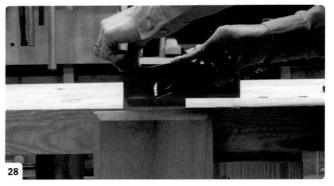

28

Guide the plane carefully to take delicate cuts. This is a fine finishing tool, not a fast tool.

29

The precisely machined side of the plane, square to the bed, gets right into the corner. Both the side and the end of the iron cut. Some people like to have the side of their iron just a hair wider than the plane, some people like to have it flush.

30

The skew block plane is ideal for cleaning up tenon faces. With the side removed, the iron fits right into the corner of the shoulder.

31

The skewed iron leaves a smooth, flat surface. Just be careful not to take off too much and not to tip the plane. Tipping results in the cheeks of the tenon being out of parallel, or may impart some twist to it.

32

The router plane offers the most control, because you can set it for a specific depth. Use another piece butted up against the end of the tenon so the plane is supported on both sides. Come in from both edges toward the middle, spinning the two workpieces around to work from the other edge. Repeating this on the other cheek guarantees that the tenon is perfectly centered.

33

This isn't as smooth as the skew block planed surface, but it has a consistent depth, with no bumps or divots, and the two surfaces are absolutely parallel.

34

To trim the tenon to width, line up the edge of the tenon with the horn line and mark where the ends of the mortise fall. Make sure all your reference marks are in the proper orientation. In particular, make sure the rail isn't flipped upside down.

35

Run lines from these marks to the shoulder.

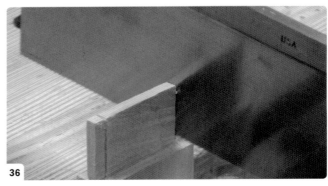

36

Stand the rail up in the vise and rip down along these lines, stopping just shy of the shoulder. This rips down very quickly, and it's easy to go too far.

37

Set the crosscut in the knifewall trough and cut off the tenon waste. This goes fast as well because it's a tiny bit of wood.

38

Lightly chamfer the end of the tenon on all four sides.

39

Dry-fit the joint. It should slip in with a little hand pressure and close up with a tight, flush line.

40

The whole assembly should lie flat.

41

The ideal result is that everything fits right off the saw. But that takes practice, and what do you do in the meantime when you need to adjust a joint? It's very tempting to pare down the walls inside the mortise with a chisel, but unless there are very obvious high spots there resist that temptation, because that can quickly get away from you. It's better to adjust the tenon using one of the above techniques, or by fine paring. Look for high spots or anything out of alignment. Every little bit of material removed risks making the joint too loose. An effective technique is to fuzz up the surface of a spot with the corner of the chisel, then shear the fuzz off. This allows you to take off very tiny amounts in very specific spots.

Drawboring

One way to deal with loose mortise-and-tenon joints is to drawbore them. This makes a joint that's almost as solid as the wood itself.

Drawboring means pinning the joint, with the hole in the tenon slightly offset from the hole in the mortise. Driving the pin through the holes draws the joint up tight.

1

To make a ¼" drawbore pin, use mallet and chisel to split the outer edge off a piece of straight-grained wood that's about ³/₈" thick. This leaves the side running parallel to the grain. Then split out a piece about ³/₈" wide.

2

The resulting ³/₈"-square pin blank is extremely strong, because the grain runs straight through its entire length.

3

Roughly sharpen the end of the pin with the chisel.

4

Using a dowel plate, drive the square pin through the ³/₈" hole. Position the hole of the plate over a dog hole, and put a bucket underneath to catch the pin.

5

Drive the pin through progressively smaller holes until it is ¼" in diameter.

6

Mark the point on the outside of the mortise that is centered, and about half the length of the tenon.

7

Put a bit of scrap in the mortise to keep the inside from splitting out, and bore a ¼" hole all the way through.

8

Slip the tenon into the mortise. Place the tip of the drill bit in the hole and spin it backward. This marks the center of the hole in the tenon without actually drilling it.

9

Pull the tenon out and mark a line about 1/32" from the drill mark, closer to the shoulder. This is the offset for the tenon hole. It must be on the shoulder side of the drill mark, not the other side. Make a cross mark on the line lined up with the drill mark.

10

Set the point of the drill at the intersection of these two marks and make a starting hole with it.

11

Put a scrap under the tenon and bore all the way through.

12

Slip the tenon into the mortise to check the alignment. The small crescent of wood visible in the lower edge of the hole is the tenon offset. That's the magic of this joint. This photo also shows a mistake to avoid. There's some side play in the joint because the tenon is a little narrower than the length of the mortise. I didn't align the edge of the rail perfectly with the line on the tenon when I marked the position of the hole with the drill bit. Therefore it will go together out of alignment when I peg it up.

13

Position the hole in the joint over a hole in the bench and insert the peg. You can glue up a drawbored joint, but it's not necessary. That's because as you drive the pin through the hole, it will flex slightly through the offset path, forming a mechanical cross lock held in place by spring tension. Here I've put glue on the tenon and on the pin.

14

Drive the peg with a mallet until it fully protrudes through the hole. The offset in the holes causes the peg to draw the joint up tight together. Hence the name of the joint, drawbore. The piece should feel completely solid immediately, without waiting for the glue to dry.

15

Flip the joint over and check the underside. The shoulder line should be tight on this side as well. If the peg wasn't sharpened enough, it can cause breakout around the edge of the hole as it comes through.

16

Saw off the excess peg on each side close to the surface.

17

Use a skewed, slicing cut with a chisel flat on the surface to flush the peg ends down, being careful not to dig into the surrounding wood.

18

The resulting joint should feel as strong as if the tree grew this way naturally. Cut off the horn and plane the stile end flush with the rail edge.

Drilling & Sawing

Using the drill-and-pare method for the mortise, and the saw-and-pare method for the tenon. Since this does not use a mallet, it can be used when you need to be quiet.

For both the mortise and the tenon, this consists of a rough step and a fine step. The rough step can be accomplished quickly, removing the bulk of the waste without having to be precise. The fine step needs to be precise, but it also goes quickly because there's very little remaining material to remove.

For the mortise, the rough step is boring with a drill. The fine step is paring the remainder to the line with a chisel.

For the tenon, the rough step is sawing about 1/16" away from the line. The fine step is paring the remainder to the line with a chisel.

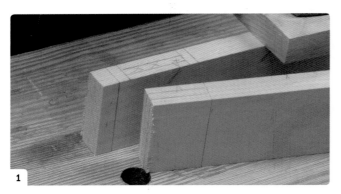

1

Lay out the parts the same as before.

2

Using a 1/4" bit, drill a series of holes in the mortise. Put a piece of masking tape on the bit to mark the depth. Be sure to keep the bit straight between the mortise walls.

Position each hole just past the last, until you get to the end of mortise.

3

To remove the remaining mortise waste, set the chisel right in the scribe line and pare straight down the wall with hand pressure. Do this for the length of the mortise.

Spin the chisel around and repeat on the other wall.

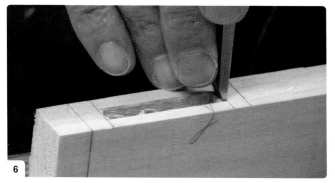

To clear the ends, set a chisel of the correct width right on the end line and pare straight down, using hand pressure. If the waste is too heavy to pare with a single stroke, do it in two or three.

Clean out the mortise with a narrow chisel.

The resulting mortise with straight walls.

Instead of sawing right to the shoulder line to make your tenon, mark about 1/16" from the line.

10

Do the same with the cheeks.

11

Set the crosscut saw on the shoulder mark and saw down to the cheek mark. Because this is not right at the shoulder, it is a rough cut.

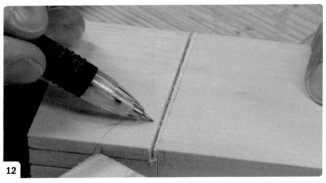

12

The completed cut. Flip the piece over and repeat for the other shoulder.

13

Make one or two additional crosscuts on each cheek, spaced so that you can use your chisel to pare off the waste.

14

Put the piece in the vise with a corner of the tenon up and use a ripsaw to cut down the corner of the cheek as before. However, position the saw at the 1/16" mark away from the gauge lines. As with the shoulder cut, this is a rough cut. Repeat for the other cheek.

15

Flip the piece over in the vise and repeat on the opposite corner. Since this is a rough cut, the kerfs from the two corners don't need to match up perfectly.

16 Stand the piece upright and saw down to the shoulder line, removing the cheek waste. Repeat on the back side.

17 The resulting rough-cut tenon. This actually cut past the additional crosscut. If that happens, you can run the crosscut saw over it a stroke or two, or deepen it with a marking knife. You can also just leave it and pare it that way if the wood is cooperative. To avoid this, make the additional crosscuts after sawing off the cheeks rather than before.

18 To remove the remaining cheek waste, with the piece upright in the vise, set the paring chisel right in the cheek scribe line and push straight across toward the middle.

19 Repeat from the other direction. The wood should curl up nicely.

20 Repeat this on the next chisel-width portion of the cheek.

21 Skew the chisel and use a sideways slicing cut to remove small parings. Spin the piece around in the vise and repeat the process on the other cheek.

This is a variation on the grip, with the thumb pulling the chisel flat against the tenon as it cuts.

Remove any remaining feathers by driving the end of the chisel with your thumb.

Mark the tenon width using the mortise as a pattern.

Rip the tenon to width at these marks. Cut down to the rough shoulder line.

Crosscut these scraps at the rough shoulder line.

To remove the remaining shoulder waste, with the piece again upright in the vise, set the corner of the paring chisel right in the shoulder scribe line and push straight across the end grain. Because just the corner is cutting, it will go through even hardwood. Use your whole body to lean into the cut, and be sure to cut in flat and level, square to the face of the piece. It doesn't have to go all the way in to the tenon on the first pass.

28

Continue using the corner to nibble across the entire shoulder, about ⅛" at a time. Once you have an initial flat cleared, you can register the flat back of the chisel on that surface, pivoting the chisel on the trailing corner to rock the leading corner into the cut. Once you get the rhythm of this down, it goes quickly and efficiently. Click the corner into place in the scribe line, register the other corner, and push into the cut. This leaves a crisp, precise shoulder edge.

29

Stand the chisel flat on the tenon cheek. Using light pressure and driving with your thumb, pare straight down that last ¹⁄₁₆" to the shoulder line. Be careful not to split into the shoulder.

30

Make a second pass, cutting in to meet the paring cut you just made to leave a crisp, precise inside corner on the shoulder. Use the surface left by the first pass to register the chisel flat.

31

Do this on the short shoulder along the thickness of the workpiece.

32

Spin the workpiece around in the vise and repeat on the other side.

33

Chamfer the end of the tenon all around so it doesn't snag going in.

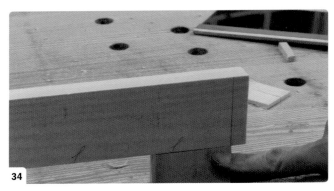

34

Fit the mortise over the tenon to check it. Here it doesn't quite bottom out. You can deepen the mortise or shorten the tenon.

35

To shorten the tenon, pare straight across from both sides to the middle. You may need to restore the chamfering.

36

Once it bottoms out, run your finger over the joint to check for twist. This tenon has just a bit.

37

Very delicately, pare off just a light shaving along the high side of the tenon on each face, using a circular shearing motion.

38

The joint goes together smoothly with light hand pressure, snug and flat.

MORTISE EXERCISE

This simple exercise consists of a series of repeated mortises. It develops your mortising skills, letting you work through mistakes without putting a project at risk. It's also useful as a warm-up to refresh your skill.

Set your marking gauge to the chisel width and run it down the length of the workpiece. Mark a random series of mortise ends across the piece, separated by at least ½". Mark X's in the waste. Darken the gauge lines with a pencil.

Chop out the first mortise.

Make as many passes as necessary to get to the desired depth.

Evaluate the mortise for mistakes. Look for damaged edges, places where the chisel twisted, and flared walls. Make a note of things to focus on. Repeat this process of chopping and evaluating with the remaining mortises.

By the time you've finished the full set, you should notice a definite improvement in your chopping. Then try it in some hardwoods. You can also do this exercise with the drill-and-pare method.

TENON EXERCISES

Sawing Exercise

The first exercise focuses on the fine sawing, using the cross-cut saw for shoulder cuts, and the ripsaw for cheek cuts.

Just as the mortising exercise consisted of a series of repeated mortises, this is a series of repeated partial tenons, cutting them off as you go.

Run gauge lines down both edges of the workpiece and darken them with a pencil. Mark the length of the tenon from the end. Anything between 1" and 2" is a good practice size.

Mark this line all around with the square and marking knife, then form a knifewall on the waste side of the line on both sides.

Make the shoulder crosscuts on both sides.

With the workpiece in the vise, run the gauge down the end grain and darken it with the pencil. Notch the corners on the waste side of each line.

Saw down the corners with the ripsaw. Repeat notching and sawing on the other corners.

Saw straight down to complete the cheek cuts and remove the cheek waste.

7

Evaluate the tenon for mistakes. Look for uneven sawing and cheeks out of parallel or out of flat. Cut this tenon off and repeat this process down the remainder of the piece.

8

By the time you've made the piece too short to continue, you should notice a definite improvement in your sawing. Then try it in some hardwoods.

Paring Exercise

The second exercise focuses on the paring for the saw-and-pare method. Instead of cutting off the tenons, you'll be repeatedly paring off the cheek and shoulder until it's too thin to work with.

1

Knife a shoulder line across the workpiece. Then, using the marking gauge registered from the back face, mark a line along the edges and across the end grain about 1/16" from the front face. This is the portion you'll be paring off for the cheek.

2

Make a pencil mark about 1/16" away from the scribed shoulder line and crosscut there down to the paring line. This leaves the portion you'll be paring off for the shoulder.

3

With the workpiece upright in the vise, set the paring chisel into the cheek scribe line.

4

Pare straight across to the middle. If this is too thick, pare it in two passes of half thickness.

5

Pare across to the middle from the other direction, removing the waste.

6

Skew the chisel and shear off any remaining fibers to get it perfectly flat.

7

Set the corner of the chisel into the shoulder scribe line and push in to pare it off. Repeat along the entire shoulder, registering the flat back of the chisel on the trimmed shoulder.

8

Pare off any remainder left on the cheek along the shoulder.

9

Evaluate the cheek and shoulder, looking for unevenness and damaged edges. Knife a new shoulder line about 1/16" from the existing shoulder. Referencing the marking gauge off the back face, mark a new cheek line along the edges and across the end grain about 1/16" from the existing cheek face. Crosscut along the shoulder down to the cheek line. Since the tenon is now getting too long to pare across with a single chisel width, make an additional crosscut to split the tenon waste into two sections.

10

Pare the two sections of the tenon. Then pare the shoulder. Repeat the process several times. The shoulder paring will go deeper with each cycle.

Stop when the remaining tenon is too thin to continue. Be careful working with the thinner tenon, because the chisel can go right through if it catches in the grain. You can cut this off and go through the whole exercise again.

THROUGH MORTISE & TENON

To make a through mortise-and-tenon joint, you mortise in from both edges to the middle. You make the tenon long enough to go all the way through with some extra margin, then trim that off and plane it flush after glue up.

The through mortise-and-tenon is a more challenging joint than the blind mortise-and-tenon, because in addition to the joint line needing to look good, you have the exposed end of the tenon on the outside. Any imperfections in your sawing or mortising on this side are going to be visible once you trim the tenon end flush.

The initial layout of the mortise on the reference edge is the same. Make sure the mortise end marks extend all the way to the reference face.

Transfer these marks to the other edge. Position the square at the first mortise end mark and make a tick mark at that position by the other edge. Repeat for the second mortise end mark.

Square those marks across the second edge.

5

Run the marking gauge between these end marks. It is critical that you run the gauge fence against the reference face, just as you did when you gauged the lines on the reference edge, to ensure that the lines are the exact same distance from that face on both edges. That ensures that any error in centering the mortise in the edge has no effect. That also allows you to position the mortise at some offset from center if you want to.

6

Mortise from the first edge down to the middle of the workpiece, leaving the ends. Then turn the workpiece over and mortise from the other edge until you are clear through.

7

Clear the ends from both edges in toward the middle.

8

Use a narrow chisel to clear out any debris.

9

Use a square to check that the ends are flat all the way through.

10

Mark the tenon to go all the way through with some extra sticking out. Other than the extra length, making this tenon is the same as a blind tenon. The only difference is that the end of the tenon will be visible, so saw it carefully. Knife the shoulder line and gauge the cheek lines.

11

Crosscut the shoulder on both faces.

12

Notch the cheek cuts and saw the cheeks with a ripsaw.

13

Mark the tenon width from the outside edge mortise length.

14

Using you finger as a fence, run those lines down the tenon.

15

Saw the tenon to width.

16

Saw off the width waste.

Slip the mortise down over the tenon with hand pressure.

17

18

With the joint seated, inspect the gap around the exposed tenon end. This has just a fingernail's thickness gap at the end, which means I trimmed it a shaving too narrow. Glue up the joint and clamp it.

19

Once the glue is dry, plane the tenon end flush. Use a block plane skewed to the cut.

20

Plane from both sides of the tenon toward the middle.

21

Check for final gaps. Minor gaps shouldn't affect the integrity of the joint.

22

Fill the gaps with glue and shavings or commercial filler, using a knife or putty knife to press it in and smooth it out.

23

After the filler is dry, trim the horn and plane the tenon end smooth.

The completed joint.

A Simple Mortising Guide

If you're having difficulty keeping the chisel straight when mortising, this is a simple guide. It's essentially half of a tenon. You can make one as part of the tenoning exercise.

Clamp the guide against the reference face of a stile at the mortise position. The depth of the guide shoulder determines where the wall of the shoulder will be relative to the reference face.

Hold the side of the chisel tight up against the guide as you strike it with the mallet.

The guide ensures that the chisel is positioned correctly along the mortise wall, and keeps it up straight. Like a sharpening jig or guide, this aids in consistency.

5

Advance the chisel along the mortise.

6

Continue using the guide to full depth. The arguments for and against it are the same as for all guided methods. The guide provides consistency, but always relying on it means you may not develop the hand skills to do without it. This is a matter of personal preferences. My preference is to train my hands to do everything unaided as much as possible. Avoiding a jig also means no fussing around with extra pieces. Guides can also be a useful aid when you need to work on a project, but you haven't yet refined your skills to the necessary level.

BRIDLE JOINT

1

A bridle joint is a cross between a lap joint and a through mortise-and-tenon. It's an open-sided, slotted mortise with through tenon. That means there are even more exposed portions of the joint, where any defects will be visible. Mostly it's an exercise in good sawing.

2

Set each piece across the other and draw pencil lines to mark rough location.

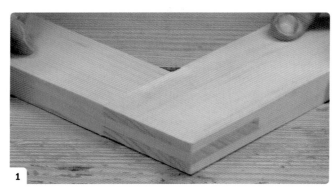

3

Knife a line at the tenon shoulder.

4

Set the knife in the scribe line and bring the square up to it.

5

Nick the other face at this position. Don't run the knife across the edge.

6

Lay the piece down, set the knife in the nick, and bring the square up to it. Knife the second shoulder line at this position.

7

Form a knifewall on the waste side of both shoulder lines.

8

Gauge cheek lines along the edges and across the end grain of both pieces. Run the gauge against the reference faces.

9

Darken the lines with pencil and mark X's in the waste. On the slotted piece, the waste is in the center, between the lines. On the tenon piece, the waste is on the outside of the lines.

10

To form the slot, notch the inside corners of the cuts. This operation is just like making a tenon, except that you are removing the center and leaving the outsides, instead of the other way around.

11

Saw down the corners with a ripsaw.

12

Flip the piece, notch the other inside corners, and saw these down.

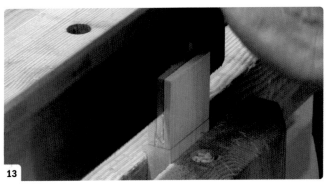

13

Stand the workpiece up in the vise and saw each cut down to the base of the slot.

14

The handle allows you to fit your other hand and thumb in to apply gentle downward force and help guide the saw. Remember to use a somewhat loose grip so that the saw tracks in the existing kerfs.

15

To remove the slot waste, set a chisel halfway down the slot, angled slightly back, and strike it with the mallet. Chop down to about halfway through. Repeat this, halving the distance to the base of the slot each time, until there is just about 1/8" left.

16

At the base of the slot, chisel straight down at the line. If there's too much to do in one pass, do it in two passes.

Flip the workpiece over and repeat on the other side.

Use a square to check that the slot is flat all the way across.

To form the tenon, notch the outside corners of the cuts. Making the tenon is exactly the same as other tenons.

The resulting pieces ready to be fitted together.

Check the fit. Like a through mortise-and-tenon, it should go together with a little friction, and the shoulder should be tight. Glue up and clamp. Clamping pressure on the slot will help close it up if it's a little too loose.

After the glue has dried, use a block plane at a skew to plane the slot end grain down, coming in from the outside of the corner.

23

Repeat on the tenon end grain.

24

Inspect the joint. This one is pretty tight on the slot end grain, but the tenon end has a large gap.

25

Fill the gaps with glue and sawdust or commercial filler.

26

After the filler has dried, plane both edges of the joint smooth, coming in from the outside of the corner.

CHAPTER 6
DOVETAIL JOINERY

DOVETAIL FIST FIGHTS & FUNDAMENTALS

After sharpening, dovetailing tends to be the biggest area of contention among woodworkers.

There are three main arguments. Should you do tails first or pins first? Should you saw out the waste or chop it out with a chisel? What angles should you use? Then there are more arguments about the fine details.

One attitude you see is, "Well, that's not the way I learned to do it, so it must be wrong." Or, "That's not how my teacher did it, and he knew what he was doing."

A better approach is to acknowledge the many teachers who have many different ways, all of which work. By learning them you develop versatility.

One thing people tend to agree about is that you should strive to fit your dovetails right off the saw. Trying to pare them to fit with a chisel afterward is mostly a losing battle, because there are so many mating surfaces that have to match, and is very time-consuming.

All of the different methods are attempting to achieve speed, efficiency and good fit, but they all present lots of opportunities for mistakes.

It's easy to get caught up in the quest for perfection, but one of the amazing things about the dovetail joint is that it has such a mechanical interlock that even a poorly fit joint will be structurally strong. You can often see evidence of this in old furniture. Surprisingly poor-fitting, inconsistent joints have still managed to survive for centuries.

The workpiece that will have the pins is the pin board, and the one that will have the tails is the tail board. The space in the pin board where a tail will fit is a tail space, and it has tail waste that must be removed. The space in the tail board where a pin will fit is a pin space, and it has pin waste that must be removed.

Good stock preparation is critical. The stock needs to be squared up and thicknessed to final dimensions, with precisely shot ends. The pin and tail boards can be the same or different thicknesses.

For through dovetails, the thickness of the pin board dictates the length of the tails, and the thickness of the tail board dictates the length of the pins.

For half-blind dovetails, the length of the tails is less than the thickness of the pin board, and the thickness of the tail board dictates the length of the pins.

In layout, the wide part of the tails must be to the outside of the joint. The tails on the tail board must flare outward to the end grain, and the tail spaces on the pin board must flare outward to the outside face. A common mistake is to orient the flare backward.

Another common mistake is to remove the pins from the pin board and leave the tail waste, or remove the tails from the tail board and leave the pin waste. To avoid this, always mark X's on the waste portion as soon as you lay it out.

It's important to maintain proper orientation of all parts. It's easy to mark one side of a joint the wrong way, or mark an entire workpiece the wrong way. Decide which face you want on the inside and outside for each side and label each part of each joint, indicating inside and outside. At every step, check these marks to make sure the workpiece is oriented properly.

Doing the tails first means forming the tail portion of the joint first, then transferring those tail shapes to the pin board and doing the pins second.

Doing the pins first means forming the pin portion of the joint first, then transferring those pin shapes to the tail board and doing the tails second.

Regardless of which workpiece you cut first, the first workpiece becomes the template for the second. So if you do tails first, that means the tail board is the template for the pins. If you do pins first, that means the pin board becomes the template for the tails.

As a result, you're really cutting the second workpiece to match the first. So if some of your angles or spacing are a little inconsistent on the first workpiece, it doesn't really matter. As long as the second workpiece matches it exactly, you'll have a good fit.

Sawing out the waste means using a coping saw to roughly saw off the bulk of the waste before finely paring the remainder with a chisel.

Chopping out the waste means using a chisel to roughly chop off the bulk of the waste before the final paring. Of the two, sawing is the quiet method, since chopping with mallet and chisel is noisy.

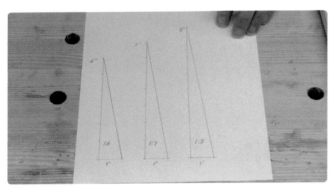

Dovetail angle refers to this angle here, and is expressed as a ratio of width to length. The choices are a 1:6 angle, a 1:7 angle, or a 1:8 angle. Some people prefer to use 1:6 angle for softwoods, and a 1:8 angle for hardwoods, while others prefer 1:7 for everything.

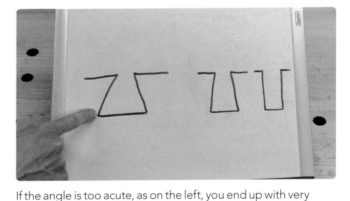

If the angle is too acute, as on the left, you end up with very weak tips. This will have too much short grain, which will break off easily. If the angle is too steep, as in the center, you don't have enough mechanical interlock, losing the inherent structural strength of the dovetail. At the extreme steepness of 90°, as on the right, it turns into a box joint.

Fundamentally, the joint consists of two parts, the tail board, left, and the pin board, right. It's called a dovetail because the outward-flaring tail shape resembles the tail of a dove. The matching pins are then what fit between those tails, typically with a half pin on each end.

The joint should go together snugly with hand pressure. If you need a lot of force to put it together, you're liable to crack something. With softwoods, compression of the fibers may allow a tight joint to come together safely, but hardwoods don't allow that compression. The end grain is a little proud so that you can flush it down to make it even with the matching face grain after glue-up.

A completed through dovetail after glue-up and trimming flush.

As with mortise-and-tenon joints, there are a variety of different types of dovetail joints. This is a half-blind dovetail, commonly used to join drawer sides to drawer fronts. The joint is visible on the side, but not on the front. As you pull the drawer from the front, the wedging action of the tails in the pins keeps the drawer from coming apart over years of use. For half-blind dovetails, you must do the tails first. They then determine how you form the sockets in the pin board.

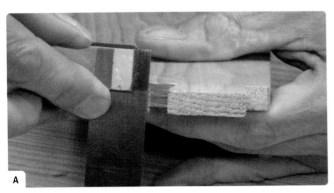

Each cut is going to have a 90° square component **(A)** and an angled component **(B)**. These tails are square across the end grain and angled along the face grain, while the matching pins are square along the face grain and angled across the end grain.

For through dovetails, the choice to remove the bulk of the waste with the saw or with the chisel is largely personal preference. Once again, however, the half-blind dovetail limits your choices. You can saw out the waste on the tail piece, but the only way to remove the socket waste on the pin piece is with a chisel, because you can't saw through the front face.

This joint is 90° at the corner and on both sides. But you can also make the joint meet at a different angle at the corner, or slope one or both sides. While a compound dovetail done at off angles in two or three dimensions sounds complex, it's no more difficult than a square one as long as you follow the fundamentals of the method.

The great strength of a dovetail comes from its complex mechanical interlock, so that even if a joint has a little play to it before it's glued up, it will be strong structurally. With no glue, this joint held at over 120 lbs, even though the wood is just soft pine.

THROUGH DOVETAILS

Good dovetails, like good mortise-and-tenon joints, rely on good layout. The layout tools are a pair of dividers, either a dovetail marker or a sliding bevel gauge, a square and a marking gauge. There are multiple ways of spacing out the dovetails. Dividers are just one way. Not shown: marking knife.

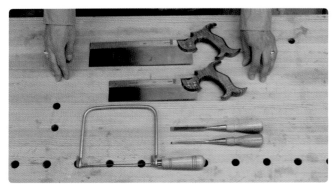

The remaining tools consist of a very fine backsaw with teeth filed in rip configuration, known as a dovetail saw, another fine backsaw in crosscut configuration, known as a carcase saw, a selection of chisels, and if you're going to saw out the waste, a coping saw.

To hold workpieces upright so you can work on the end grain easily, you can use something like this shop-built removable vise.

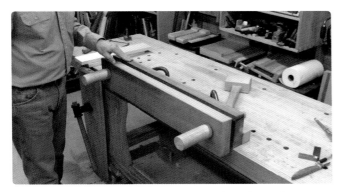

Known as a "Moxon vise," it's secured to the workbench with holdfasts or clamps.

Creating the Tails

1

Set the marking gauge to thickness of the stock. Then open it up about one shaving thicker; that way the joint ends will be slightly proud so you can plane them down flush. These workpieces are identical thickness, so one gauge setting works for both. For different thicknesses, you'll need to use different settings for tails vs. pins. The stock needs to be precisely squared up, with precisely shot ends. This dovetail will be tails first, sawing out the waste with a coping saw, laid out using a dovetail marker that's set for a 1:6 slope. Mark which piece will be the tail board and which will be the pin board.

2

Scribe the baseline on the tail board, butting the gauge tightly against the end grain. Scribe this line all around the board, on both faces and edges. Since these are the same thickness, scribe the same baseline on the pin board. However, only scribe the faces, not the edges. If the workpieces are different thickness, scribe the thickness of the pin board on the tail board, and the thickness of the tail board on the pin board.

3

You can lay out the tail spacing with dividers. These have two adjustments. The thumbscrew is a coarse adjustment, allowing you to close them down or open them wide. Once you lock that down, the knurled knob on the left is a fine adjustment, allowing you to dial it up or down by a few turns, or even as small as a quarter turn.

4

Mark the width of the half-pins on each edge of the tail board end grain and square lines across. Set the dividers on one line, opened to an approximate position. If you want three tails, set the dividers roughly to one third the width of the board. If you want five tails, set them for one fifth, and so forth. This process works for any number of regularly spaced tails.

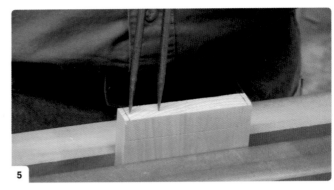

5

Walk the points of the dividers across the end grain, stepping off the desired number of tails to see where the last point ends up.

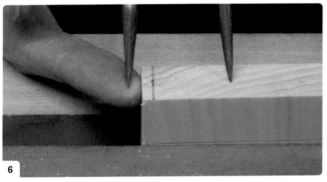

6

The desired ending position is equal to the half-pin width past the edge. If the last step ends up short of that, open the dividers up. If it falls past that, close them down. Repeat the step-off and adjustment procedure until the point finishes at the right position. A variation of this adjustment process is to start the dividers at one edge, and step off until they end up at the other edge.

7

Starting from the first half-pin mark, step off the dividers for the desired number of pins, pushing into the end grain enough to mark it. Mark these points with a pencil.

8

Starting from the second half-pin mark, step off the dividers in the other direction. This marks out the opposite side of each tail position.

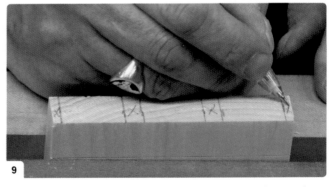

9

Square all these positions across the end grain. Mark X's in the pin spaces. Do this now before you lose track and accidentally remove the good wood instead of the waste. The inner pin spaces are twice the width of the outer half-pin spaces, no measuring required.

10

If you don't have a dovetail marker, you can use a sliding bevel gauge set to the desired angle to mark the tails. Position it at the lines you marked across the end grain.

11

If you have a marker, position it at the lines and mark along the side to the scribed baseline. Mark each tail on left and right sides, so that the tails spread out at the end grain.

12

Mark the far side of the last tail.

13

The tails laid out ready for sawing, with X's marked in the pin waste on the face of the board. You'll saw all the tail cuts with the saw tipped to the right side, then all the cuts tipped to the left.

14

The sawing stance is important. Stand so that as you have the saw tipped to one side or the other, your arm clears your body. You don't want to be so far to the side that your arm is out sideways, or so close that you're bumping into yourself. Find a comfortable position where you can sight down over the back of the saw and the teeth to the line that you're cutting.

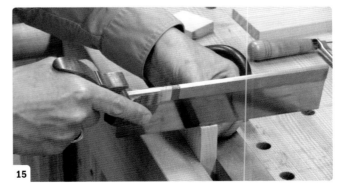

15

Place your off-hand thumbnail right at the line marked across the end and position the dovetail saw against it. The saw has to be square across the end grain, tipped over to the right at the dovetail angle.

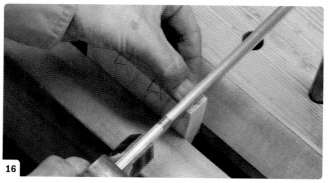

16

Sight down the back of the saw, across the saw plate, along the angled line. This alignment of the saw straight across and pitched over along the dovetail angle is critical. Whatever angles you end up with on the tail board cuts will be the template you must follow when you make the pin board cuts. Remember to use a slightly loose grip, not a tight death grip, for best control.

17

Maintaining this alignment, draw the saw back to establish the kerf. Draw it back an additional stroke or two as necessary.

18

Start sawing with steady, full-length strokes. You only have a couple strokes where you can correct anything. Once the teeth are fully in the kerf, you're committed to the cut. Use light pressure, allowing the weight of the saw to provide all the downward force. You're actually almost lifting it out of the cut as you move, to let it float through the cut lightly. Your focus should be on smooth control with a steady rhythm. Don't worry about speed. That will come with practice.

19

Saw down to the scribed baseline, but not past it.

20

Advance to the next cut at that angle. Set your thumb against the line, set the saw against it, draw back to form a kerf, and start sawing.

21

Continue with the next one. This is the view from the back side of the workpiece.

22

Once all the cuts tipped to the right are complete, tip the saw to the left dovetail angle and saw the left side of the first tail using the same procedure.

23

Advance to the next cut at that angle.

24

Rear view of the left angled cuts.

25

Inspect the workpiece from the front side. If you didn't cut exactly to the line anywhere, it doesn't really matter, because this piece will form the template for the pin piece. That's where you'll have to match these angles exactly.

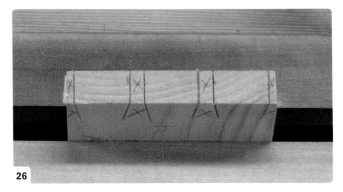

26

Inspect it from the top. This is the critical portion on this workpiece. These cuts need to be exactly 90° across the end grain. If it's a little bit out, such as the leftmost cut on this workpiece, you can get by, especially in softwood, but if it's too far out, it won't go together. That off angle will act as a wedge and jam it up tight or split the pin board before the joint closes up all the way home.

27

Use the coping saw to rough out the pin waste. The simplest way is to saw down the middle of the pin, turn the saw as you get near the bottom, and take it down to about 1/16" from the baseline, all the way to the side cut. Remove the bit of waste that pops loose.

28

Turn the saw over and saw straight across ¹⁄₁₆" from the baseline.

29

Continue with the remaining full pin spaces the same way.

30

Remove the half-pin using a small crosscut joinery saw. With the workpiece mounted edge-up, first chisel in toward the line to remove a small chip, forming a knifewall trough.

31

Set the saw up against the knifewall and carefully saw down exactly along the baseline to the dovetail cut. Alternatively, you can saw just a bit away from the baseline, and pare down across the end grain with a chisel to get right to the baseline.

32

The workpiece ready for final paring to the baseline. A narrower chisel focuses the cutting force on a smaller area, while a wider chisel provides a larger bearing surface to ensure a flat cut. Don't try to pare all the way from front to back; pare halfway in to the center from each side. That prevents blowing out on the far side. You may be able to do it with hand pressure, or you may need to use a mallet.

33

There are several ways of doing this. The first is completely unguided, with the workpiece laying down on the bench. Set the chisel in the baseline, hold it straight up, and pare down. If the waste is too thick, you can do it in two passes. You can also do this paring with the workpiece mounted upright in a vise.

34

The other method is guided, using a jointed edge up against the baseline as a vertical guide. Set the chisel in the baseline, register the back up against the guide edge, and pare down. Like the unguided method, you can also do it in two passes.

35

Using the guided method on the first pin space, holding the chisel tight up against the guide.

36

Using the unguided method on the second pin space, holding the chisel vertical by eye.

37

Flip the workpiece over. Using the guided method on the other side to complete the first space.

38

Using the unguided method on the other side to complete the second space.

39

If you have a hump in the middle because your chisel wasn't quite vertical, you can do some cleanup paring with the work-piece mounted upright, using a narrow chisel.

40

Choke up on it so it can only go halfway in. That way you don't risk breaking out the far edge. With the very tip and corner of the chisel, pare the hump flat using small circular motions. Spin the workpiece around and work from the other side as well if necessary.

41

Check for high spots with a square. It should rest on the baseline on both the front and back sides of the workpiece, in each pin space.

Making the Matching Pins

1

With the tails cut, transfer their pattern to the end grain of the pin board, and mount it upright in the vise. Flush it up level with a plane resting on its side to act as a support for the far end of the tail board.

2

Flush the edge of the tail board to the edge of the pin board, with the baseline right up against the pin board. Because you gauged the baseline a shaving longer than the pin board thickness, the ends of the tails extend proud of the pin board by a shaving. The positioning of the tail board here is critical. If the baseline is away from the pin board, the joint will be loose. If it is over the pin board end grain, the joint won't go together.

3

With the tip of the marking knife, carefully mark the outlines of the tails on the pin board end grain. This will leave faint but distinct knife lines in the grain.

4

Mark X's in the waste of the tail spaces. While not visible in the grain in this orientation in the photo, both sides of each tail are marked.

5

With the workpiece mounted for sawing, outside face toward you, square down the ends of the lines.

6

Sawing down the pins is just like sawing down the tails, except that now you need to follow the angle of the knife line exactly. Because you marked these lines on the outside of the tails, they actually delineate the very edge of the pins. Therefore you need to saw just to the waste side of the knife lines. Don't saw right on the knife lines, or the joint will be too loose. Place the saw so that the kerf is in the waste, on the outside of the knife lines. Do this by placing your thumbnail right at the line, and placing the saw against your thumbnail.

7

Repeat for all the cuts angled to the right, using a loose grip, not a death grip. Draw the saw back for a couple of strokes to establish the kerf, then saw smoothly with full strokes.

8

Rear view, make all the cuts angled to the left.

9

Inspect the workpiece from the front side. Everything should be square to the edge down to the baseline, not past the baseline. Like the square portions on the tail board, these are critical to the joint going together.

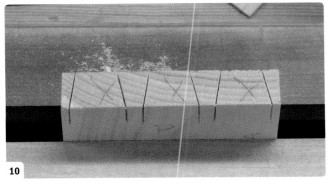

10

Inspect it from the top, making sure that each cut is right along the knife line. These are as critical as the square portions.

Saw out the tail waste with the coping saw. Saw down the middle of the waste and turn the saw near the baseline, leaving about ¹⁄₁₆" of waste. As you come up to the cut on the side, angle the saw to match the dovetail angle.

Reverse the saw and saw across the baseline, angling the saw at the end to match the dovetail angle.

Repeat for the remaining tail spaces.

Using a chisel, pare to the baseline as with the tail piece. The main differences here are that you can use a wider chisel, and you have to tip the chisel sideways along each pin to match the dovetail angle. Use multiple passes if the wood is too heavy to do it in a single pass, with or without a mallet.

You can do this with the guided method as well.

Flip the piece over and repeat on the back side, using the unguided method...

17

...or the guided method.

18

Mount the workpiece upright and do final delicate paring of any hump with a narrow chisel, choked up on the end so it only goes halfway across. Use a circular, shearing cut.

19

Finish off from the other side, shearing from the edge to the middle.

20

Test the fit. Use your fist to set it, or put a scrap across the tails and tap it down with a mallet. It should take a little pressure to go together, but not so much that you have to hammer it in. Heavy hammering will most likely cause something to split. If it only goes a little way then sticks, check all the square cuts to make sure none are flared out, acting as a wedge to prevent them from seating all the way. You can lightly pare the high portion of such spots to square them up, but this type of adjustment can rapidly go too far.

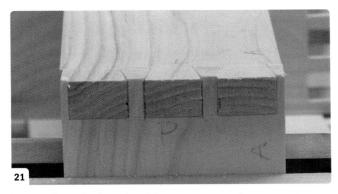

21

Inspect from the front. Look for gaps or out-of-square cuts.

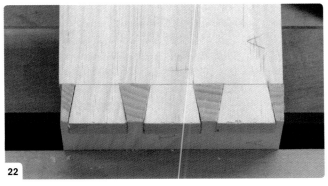

22

Inspect from the top. Look for gaps or mismatched angles.

23

The ends of the pins and tails are slightly proud of the surface. You'll plane these down flush after the glue has dried. This tail board is also slightly wider than the pin board, so that edge will need to be planed flush.

24

Use a glue brush to spread glue on the sides of the pins and tails. You can put glue on the end grain at the base of each socket as well, but it won't contribute much to the strength of the joint. Assemble and clamp the joint.

25

After the glue dries, clamp the assembly for flushing up the joint. Since you'll normally be building a complete box shape, not just one joint, secure a support board to the workbench and hang the joint over it. Reorient the assembly as necessary to work each side of each joint.

26

Using a fine-set plane held skewed to the cut, plane straight in from the edge. Flush the pin ends down to the surface of the tail board.

27

Reorient the assembly to flush the tail ends down to the surface of the pin board.

28

The completed joint. The small gaps visible during dry fit have closed up some, due to the moisture of the glue swelling the wood a bit.

Variation: Starting With the Pins

1

This dovetail will be pins-first, chiseling out the waste rather than sawing it out. Starting with squared-up stock that has precisely shot ends, scribe a baseline all the way around the tail board with the marking gauge, and just on the faces of the pin board.

2

On the outside face of the pin board, mark half pins ⅛" in from each edge. Square these down from the end to the baseline.

3

Step out the pins and tails on this face exactly the way you stepped them out on the end grain of the tail board when you did tails first.

4

Square those lines down to the baseline.

5

Mount the workpiece upright and with a dovetail marker or sliding bevel gauge set to the dovetail angle, mark the angle sides of the pins on the end grain. You can square the ends down the back face, but it's not necessary.

6

Mark X's in the tail waste. Make sure you've marked the end grain so that the tails flare out toward you.

7

Saw out the pins exactly as before, angled across the end grain and straight down the face. Place your thumbnail at the line, place the saw against your thumbnail, and draw back two strokes to establish the kerf. Then saw down to the baseline smoothly with a loose grip.

8

Repeat for all the cuts at this angle.

9

Switch to the other angle and make all those cuts.

10

Secure the pin board flat on the bench for chopping the waste. There are two general approaches, and either one can be done guided or unguided at the baseline.

11

The first approach is to do rough chopping about 1/16" from the baseline, remove the bulk of the waste, then come back and do fine paring at the baseline. This is very similar to doing rough sawing, then paring the remainder. Since this is rough, you can chop deeply using the mallet.

12

Make angled relief chops in the waste and lever out the chips.

13

Carefully come in from the front and chip off a thick layer. Repeat the steps of straight chop, angled chop, and chipping off until you're halfway down.

14

Flip the piece over and repeat the rough chopping steps until you cut all the way through. You can't chip up from the front on this side because of the sloping sides of the pins.

15

Set the chisel in the baseline and pare the remainder down halfway.

16

Flip the piece back over and pare at the baseline from this side, angling the chisel along the pins.

17

The second approach is to do all the work right at the baseline. This allows you to skip the rough chopping step, but requires a little more care in the initial chopping. Set the chisel in the baseline and chop down very lightly. Too heavy a chop will result in the bevel pushing the chisel back past the baseline.

18

Cut in at an angle to remove a small chip. Now there is a deep enough shoulder at the baseline to chop down more heavily. Repeatedly chop down, then cut in at angle to deepen the cut until it is halfway through. Instead of chipping in from the front, leave that waste to support the piece when you flip it over.

Repeat these steps on each tail space. For efficiency, repeat each cut on all the spaces before changing to the next cut. Chop all the spaces at the baseline, then come back and cut in at an angle on all the spaces.

Flip the piece over and repeat the process from the other side until the scraps come loose.

Mount the workpiece upright and pare the spaces lightly.

Choke up on the end of the chisel and pare in from both sides in to the middle.

Use a square to check that the spaces are flat with no humps, so that the tails will seat down fully in them.

Making the Matching Tails

1 The pin board is the template for marking the tail piece. Stand the pin board up on end on the inside face of the tail board, with the inside edge lined up on the tail board baseline. Make sure the flare of the tails is outward, with the wide part of the tails at the end grain. Run the marking knife alongside the pin ends.

2 This leaves faint knife lines at the edges of the tails. Mark X's in the waste. Run the pencil down the knife lines to darken them.

3 Mount the workpiece upright and square the ends of the lines across the end grain.

4 Mark X's in the end grain waste.

5 When you saw these out, it's critical that you saw on the waste side of these lines, in the X space. That means you'll leave the knife lines and half the width of the pencil lines.

6 Since this is the tail board, you'll saw straight across, with the saw tipped to the side. Put your thumbnail on the line and the saw against your thumbnail. Sight down over the back of the saw to line it with the knife line at the dovetail angle. Draw back a couple of strokes to establish the kerf, then saw smoothly with a loose grip.

7

Continue with the remaining cuts at this angle.

8

Tip the saw to the other side, align it with the knife line at the dovetail angle, and do all the cuts to that side.

9

Inspect the cuts for squareness across, and alignment with the knife lines.

10

To remove the half-pin waste, use a chisel to take out a chip in the waste at the baseline.

11

Carefully saw off the half-pin waste.

12

If there are some fibers left behind, cut straight down with a chisel to remove them. Repeat this process on the other half-pin space.

13

Removing the pin waste is the same as removing the tail waste on the pin board. Try doing this first space initially chopping away from the baseline, and the other one at the baseline. Set the chisel away from the baseline and chop down with a mallet. Because you're away from the baseline, you can be quite aggressive. Make sure the chisel is narrower than the pin space at this position.

14

Angle in to remove a chip. Repeatedly chop down, then in, to deepen this until it is halfway through.

15

Do this one at the baseline. Set the chisel in the baseline. Because you're at the baseline, you have to very gently tap down to avoid pushing back past it.

16

Angle in to remove a small chip. Repeat this light tap and small chip until the shoulder is established, then you continue with heavier strikes and chips until you're halfway through.

17

Turn the workpiece over. Finish the space that you did at the baseline. Repeat the process of two gentle taps and small chips, then work more heavily until you're all the way through.

18

Finish the space that you did away from the baseline. Repeat the process of heavy chops and chips until you're all the way through.

19 For the final bit of waste, set the chisel in the baseline and pare straight down to halfway through. Do it in two passes if the wood is too heavy to pare all at once.

20 Turn the workpiece over again, set the chisel in the baseline, and pare off the remaining waste. These variations of chopping away from the baseline or right at it, with or without a guide, offer a lot of flexibility in the way you do this. You can apply the appropriate speed and control for the situation. A hardwood drawer for a fine jewelry box is different from a rough pine storage bin.

21 Mount the workpiece upright and do final precision paring to clean out the spaces, choking up on the chisel and working from both sides into the middle.

22 The joint should go together smoothly with a bit of friction. Drive it down with your fist, or lay a scrap across the tails and tap it down with a mallet. Don't force it, that will cause something to crack.

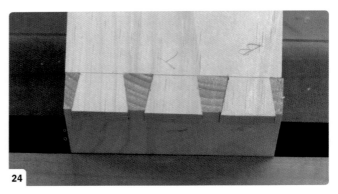

23 Inspect the joint from the front and sides.

24 Inspect it from the top.

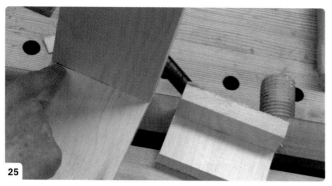

25

Inspect the inside as well. This one has some gaps at the baseline on the left two spaces. This is most likely from tapping too hard with the mallet, causing the chisel to push back past the line. The method of chopping away from the baseline avoids this, at the cost of an additional step to pare the remaining waste. The previous joint, on the right, has no gaps.

26

Glue up the joint.

27

After the glue has dried, flush up the ends of the pins and tails with a fine-set smooth plane.

28

The final joint. Both pins-first and tails-first produced identical results.

DOVETAIL SAWING EXERCISE

The secret to good dovetails is good sawing. This exercise develops that skill by repetitively making the cuts that form dovetails. The repetition allows your brain, your eye, and your hand to dial in the control. First do it with softwood like pine, then do it in hardwood.

This is also a good warm-up exercise to prepare for a project after you haven't done it for a while.

1 A

1 B

Every dovetail joint has four cuts to it. **(A)** The tail cuts are straight across the end grain and pitched to the left or the right on the face grain. **(B)** The pin cuts are angled to the left or right across the end grain, and straight down on the face grain.

Mount a practice piece upright and scribe baselines front and back on the end.

Using a dovetail marker or sliding bevel gauge, mark several angled tail cuts in each direction on the face grain, and several angled pin cuts in each direction on the end grain.

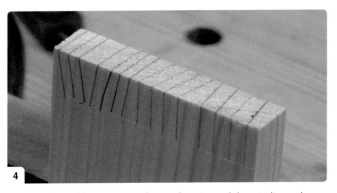

Square the tail lines across the end grain and the pin lines down the face grain. Turn the workpiece around and mark the corresponding lines on the other face.

Make each set of repeated cuts. Place your thumbnail on the line, the saw against your thumbnail, and draw back a couple of strokes to establish the kerf. Then saw in smooth, full strokes with a loose grip. As you complete each cut, inspect it on both faces to see how well it tracked on the front, across the top, and on the back. Check that it doesn't go past the baseline on either side. As you see a problem with a cut, focus on correcting that on the next cut.

Cut the workpieces off at the baseline, shoot the end grain, and repeat the whole process. Do four repetitions, giving you a dozen tries at each cut.

HALF-BLIND DOVETAILS

Half-blind dovetails are commonly used to join thin drawer sides to thick drawer fronts, so that there's no joint visible on the front side. The side is the tail board, and the front is the pin board.

Because the tail board will act as the template for making the sockets in the pin board, this is by definition a tails-first joint. However, layout begins with the pin board, because you need to know how deep to make those sockets across the end grain. They don't go all the way to the front.

Mount the pin board upright so that the front face is away from you. Make a pencil mark measured from the front indicating where you want the tails to end. This one is ¼" from the front face. With the marking gauge fence against the back face, set it to that mark and scribe a line across the end grain.

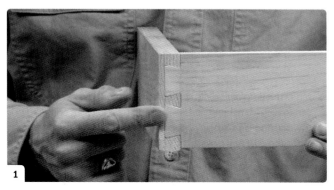

Scribe this setting as the baseline around the faces and edges at the end of the tail board.

Set the marking gauge to the thickness of the tail board.

Scribe this setting as the baseline on the back face of the pin board. Don't mark the front face or the edges.

Mount the tail board upright and step out the tails just as for a through dovetail.

7

Square those lines across the end grain.

8

With a dovetail marker or sliding bevel gauge, mark the dovetail angles on the face.

9

Mark X's in the waste. Check that the tails are flaring outward to the end of the board.

10

Saw the tails exactly the same as for a through dovetail. Place you thumbnail at the line, and the saw against your thumbnail. Tip the saw over at the dovetail angle, sighting down across the back and aligning it to the angled pencil line. Draw two light strokes back to establish the kerf, then saw smoothly with a loose grip. Saw all the lines pitched to the right, then all the lines pitched to the left.

11

Mount the workpiece edge-up and remove a small chip in the waste at the baseline.

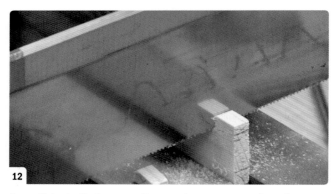

12

Saw off the half-pin waste. Repeat these steps on the other half-pin.

13

Remove the pin waste by one of the methods for through dovetails.

14

Do final paring of the pin spaces.

15

Mount the pin board upright and use a plane on its side to support the tail board for marking.

16

Line up the end of the tail board with the line scribed in the end of the pin board. Carefully scribe along the tails to mark out the pins on the pin board.

17

Darken the knife lines with a pencil. Square the lines down the inside face of the pin board to the baseline. Mark X's in the waste.

18

Sawing the pins presents a new challenge, because you can't saw through the front. The front face of the drawer needs to be pristine, with no marks on it. There are two strategies. The first is to saw diagonally across the inside corner only as far as the baseline and front line allow you to go. This is a very small cut along the side of the pin. As with through dovetails, saw to the waste side of the line, in the tail waste.

19

The second is to saw down past the baseline while stopping at the front line. This leaves extended cuts on the inside of the drawer face, but no one will ever see them unless they pull the drawer out and look at that face. This is actually a historically accurate method, fairly common in antique furniture. It allows the cut along the side of the pin to go further.

20

Secure the workpiece for chopping out the tail waste. The far space has only been sawn as far as the baseline, while the other two have been sawn past the baseline.

21

Roughly chop the tail waste about 1/16" away from the baseline in all the spaces.

22

Chip up from the front. Do this carefully, because these chips will come off easily. Repeat this process of chopping down and chipping up until you're down close to the scribe line.

23

Do the remainder very carefully, a thin layer at a time. Alternately pare down at the baseline and in from the front. Leave the last layer of fibers along the front line.

24

Mount the workpiece upright and remove the last layers by paring straight down. Do this along the walls as well to clean out the corners.

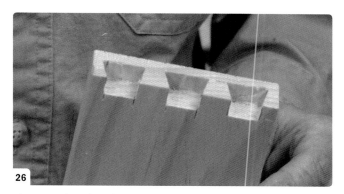

25 The very bottoms of the corners are often difficult to clean out. Use a narrow chisel to get in and remove a few fibers at a time. Choke up on the chisel to avoid pushing it through the front face. You can also scrape with the point of the chisel. This is very fine, delicate detail work. Don't rush it.

26 The completed pin board.

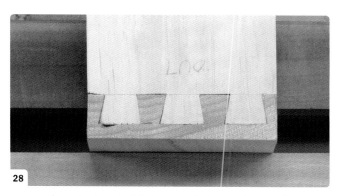

27 Test the fit and inspect to see that the tails are flush in their sockets.

28 Inspect from the top. A little too much chipped out while excavating the tail space on the left. The left half-pin shoulder on the tail board is also angled. Though unsightly, small defects like these should not affect the joint.

29 Glue up the joint, applying glue in the sockets and along the tails. Fill any gaps with glue and sawdust or commercial filler.

30 After the glue dries, flush up the joint using a fine-set smoothing plane held at a skew.

The completed joint.

SLIDING DOVETAILS

The sliding dovetail is a specialized version of a dado. It's a groove across the grain.

The walls of the dado angle in, forming a long dovetail socket. The end of the mating piece is a long tail that slides into the socket.

Make two pencil marks to mark the width of the tail piece. Bring those around the edge with a square.

Set the marking gauge to the depth of the socket and roll it across between the marks. Darken the scribe line with a pencil. Leave the gauge at this setting for marking the tail piece later.

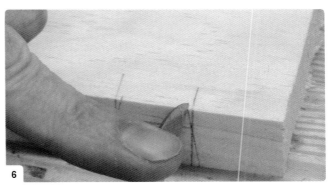

Using a dovetail marker or sliding bevel gauge set to 1:6 angle, mark the dovetail angles across the edge. The angled line crosses the intersection of the vertical and horizontal lines.

With the end of the marking knife, make a tick mark on the top face at the end of each angled line.

The completed marking at the end of the socket.

Square those marks across the face. Set the knife tip in the tick mark, butt the square against the front edge and slide it over to meet the knife, then scribe across.

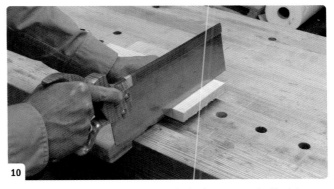

Form a knifewall trough on the waste side of each scribe line.

Saw across this just like a regular dado, but instead of holding the saw up square, tip it over at the dovetail angle. Use the angled line on the edge as a sight line to align it. Sight down across the back of the saw to the far end of the line.

11

The saw pitched over, aligned with the marks. The knifewall trough puts the saw kerf on the waste side of the line. Saw with smooth strokes down to the depth mark.

12

Saw the other side with the saw tipped the other way.

13

The finished cuts.

14

Roll up the waste at the end with a chisel. Start at half depth, then half the remaining depth each time until you're down to the scribe line.

15

Repeat on the other end.

16

Roll up the remainder in the middle, coming in from each end.

17

Set a router plane to the depth for final precise excavation.

18

Route in from both ends toward the middle. For tough spots, it helps to anchor one side of the router with one hand and pivot the tool with the other hand. That provides leverage to get through the cut.

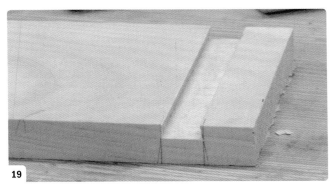

19

The completed socket.

20

Mark the tail piece. The end must be precisely shot. Run the gauge across the end on each face. Make several passes to form a good line. This is actually cutting the shoulder of the dovetail.

21

Deepen the gauge lines with the marking knife. This is all the crosscutting that's required on this small shoulder. If you need to make a deeper shoulder, form a knifewall trough on the waste side of the line and saw to depth, straight down.

22

This is a simple chisel guide for cutting the dovetail angle in the end grain. It's just a jointed board that has been planed down at the dovetail angle along one side.

23

To set up the guide, secure it to the bench. Secure the workpiece with the end grain parallel to the guide, positioned so that when you run the chisel straight down the guide, it just meets the end of the face, at both the near corner and the far corner. If the guide isn't thick enough, put a spacer board underneath it to raise it up.

24

The chisel should contact the workpiece right at the corner. The guide is on top of a piece of plywood as a spacer to make things line up properly.

25

To cut the dovetail, run the chisel down the guide and into the end grain.

26

Continue this across the entire width of the piece.

27

You can also run the chisel along the edge, peeling up a shaving. Do this a few layers of wood at a time, delicately to avoid damaging the shoulder, until you have cut the full depth.

28

If necessary, run the knife along the shoulder to free the shavings.

29 Turn the piece over and align it to the guide. Secure it to the bench.

30 Run the chisel in on this side and trim off the shavings with the knife.

31 The completed tail after removing the last remnants of shavings.

32 Fit the tail into the socket and slide it in as far as you can.

33 This joint has a lot of friction, especially if either piece is at all out-of-flat. Put a scrap over the edge and carefully drive the piece home with a mallet.

34 Inspect the front. This fits well, though the very corner of the tail has been dented. But that can be filled easily.

35 Inspect the shoulder on each side.

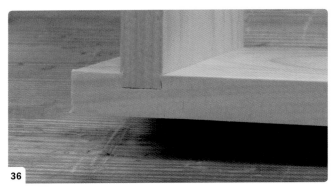

36 Inspect the back. This is not quite as snug, but it still offers a good mechanical interlock.

Tapered Sliding Dovetails

1 A tapered sliding dovetail is a minor variation. The layout is the same, except that the far end of one of the lines is moved in about 1/8". That will form the taper in the socket.

2 Mark the same taper in the end grain of the tail piece. That will form the taper in the tail.

3 Make sure the tail piece is oriented properly so that the desired face is aligned to the taper when you stand it upright.

4 Sawing the socket is the same as the non-tapered joint, except that one side will be out-of-square across the face, at the taper angle.

5 Chiseling the socket is also the same. Just make sure the chisel fits in the narrow end of the taper.

6 Routing the socket is exactly the same.

7 The completed tapered socket.

8 The biggest difference is in the guide setup. Skew the piece relative to the guide so that the chisel follows the taper along the guide.

9 At the wide end of the taper, the chisel contacts the piece at the corner of the end grain.

10 At the narrow end, through the magic of compound geometry, skewing the piece out-of-parallel causes the chisel to contact the piece at the taper line. It does so all along the line.

Run the chisel along the taper, raising chips. Make deeper passes at the narrow end. Then run the chisel all along it for a final pass.

Run the knife along the shoulder to cut off the chips, making deeper passes at the narrow end.

On the non-tapered side, set up and form the same as a non-tapered joint, with the end of the tail piece parallel to the guide.

The result is a dovetail-keyed end, tapering to a deeper key at the back edge.

The tail slides easily into the socket until the end.

The last bit takes hand pressure to slide home.

17

Inspect the front. This one is a bit loose, showing the challenge of cutting the taper exactly. One way to avoid that is to leave it a little fat until final fitting, then sneak up on it a shaving at a time, repeatedly testing the fit.

18

Inspect the back end.

19

Inspect the shoulders along the joint.

20

One of the features of the tapered sliding dovetail is that you can easily take it apart. A little gentle persuasion from your fist or a mallet knocks the tail loose, then you can slide it out.

This makes the joint suitable for knock-down furniture that you can assemble and disassemble repeatedly. Over time the joint may loosen up with repetition, so make it heavy enough, out of strong enough wood, to withstand that use. It's also suitable for one-time on-site assembly, then you can glue it up.

21

CHAPTER 7

BORING HOLES & CURVED WORK

BORING HOLES

The tools for boring holes consist of braces in various styles, bits, eggbeater drills, push drills, gimlets and awls.

Braces are the real workhorses here, because they have the power to drive large bits. The size of a brace is measured by its sweep, which is the diameter of the circle swept out by the brace, or its throw, which is the radius of that circle. Throw is measured from the centerline of the handle to the centerline of the bit axis. Left to right, a wooden 7" Sheffield brace, an 8" Spofford brace, a 10" ratchet brace, and a 12" Spofford brace. That means a 3½" throw, a 4" throw, a 5" throw, and a 6" throw.

Throw is a measure of the lever arm on a brace. The larger the throw, the more leverage you get out of the brace as you're rotating it. Either one of these Spofford braces would drive a small bit, but the larger one on the right would drive a large one more easily.

A ratcheting brace, right, can be used in tighter spaces where there isn't room for the full sweep, but a simpler brace is lighter and less cumbersome. The Spofford brace, left, is one of my favorite tools, because the markings date it to just after the time that Abraham Lincoln was president, and it works beautifully. When I need to bore a hole, it's my tool of first choice.

There are a variety of chucking mechanisms, from the simple thumbscrew on the Spofford brace, with a square drive, to the more complex chuck on the ratcheting brace, and the simple square drive with latch on the wooden Sheffield brace. The chuck on the ratcheting brace can also take modern hexagonal bits.

A Russell Jennings pattern bit. From the right end, the functional parts are the square drive, the auger, the flukes, the cutting lip and the lead screw. These come in sets in 1/16" increments, with the number of sixteenths stamped into the square drive end, from 4 to 16.

The flukes consist of sharp cutting points that scribe out the circle. The cutting lip then excavates the waste and sends it up the auger, which is an Archimedean screw. The lead screw actually pulls the bit through the wood so you don't have to apply pressure.

Because of the lead screw, you apply just enough pressure on the pad of the brace to keep it upright. You just provide the rotational power, the bit does the work of pulling itself through the wood.

As you turn the brace, the lead screw pulls the bit in, the flukes scribe out the circle, and the cutting lip pulls out the waste. Stop when the screw just pokes through the bottom. Turn the piece over, set the screw in the hole from the other side, and bore out the remainder of the hole. The lead screw will quickly run out of wood to pull it, but with a little bit of pressure the flukes will cut through. The result is a clean hole on both sides.

On the ratcheting brace, turn the ratchet collar to the desired position. When centered, the ratchet is locked in neutral and will drive the bit when turning the brace forward or reverse. When set to one side, the ratchet is locked for forward use. Reversing the brace, the bit doesn't turn. When set to the other side, the ratchet is locked for reverse use. Turning the brace forward, the bit doesn't turn.

The ratchet action allows you to move the brace back and forth in a small arc to advance or reverse the bit, such as when working inside a corner or other restricted space. The mechanism needs a little resistance in the wood to grip the bit on the return stroke, so you may need to put a little more pressure on the pad. This can make it a little finicky to get started. The lead screw on the bit still does its work.

Precision boring requires two things: a precise location, and straight alignment. To locate a bit precisely on a mark, use an awl to bore a small starter hole for the point of the bit.

For alignment, set two squares 90° to each other. Set the point of the bit in the starter. Align the bit so that it's parallel to the squares in each axis. Keep it aligned as you turn, sighting straight down it and from the sides. You can make major corrections within the first few turns. After that, focus on keeping it straight and steady to avoid a wobbly hole.

To make an angled hole, align it to a sliding bevel gauge. For compound angles, such as for chair legs, use two bevel gauges.

You can also bore horizontally. It's easy to see if the brace is square to the piece in the horizontal plane looking down on it, but how can you tell if it's square vertically?

Use the ring trick. Put a wedding band or other ring on the shaft of the bit. As you turn, if the bit is horizontal, it will stay in that spot. Otherwise, the ring will wander forward or back along the shaft. This is less precise than sighting along a square, but is effective in a pinch.

You can also use older square-drive bit designs, such as spoon bits and this center-spur bit.

The outer spur scores the wood and the cutting lip excavates the waste scored. But because it doesn't have a lead screw, you have to apply downward pressure to advance it. This style isn't nearly as efficient as the previous one.

There are also antique specialty bits, like these spiral and fluted countersinks. The other common bit is the slotted screw driver.

Eggbeater drills work with modern twist bits for smaller holes. Some have selectable high- and low-speed gears. The handle is hollow for bit storage.

The high gear ratio and relatively long handle create fast revolutions with good torque. The key to using these efficiently is to use a sharp bit, without putting too much downward pressure on the drill. Let the bit do its job. A couple of drops of oil in the oil holes on the body can perform an amazing transformation on a stiff and balky tool.

A push drill is another efficient method for making small holes. It uses special bits that are stored in the handle. You can still buy replacement bits for these.

It works with a pumping action. Push down to drive it, and the spring inside pushes it back up.

Gimlets are simply spiral bits with a handle.

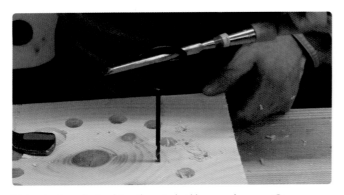

Twist the handle to drive the gimlet like a corkscrew. Open-handle styles allow you to slip a chisel or other long lever in to get better leverage. This is also easier on your hand. Gripping and twisting a gimlet can be uncomfortable.

Awls are the simplest boring tools. Left is a bradawl, and right is a birdcage awl. The bradawl is intended for softwoods. The birdcage awl works in hardwoods. These work well for making starter holes and small pilot holes.

The bradawl, used for making pilot holes for brads, has a chisel tip. Orient the chisel across the grain and press. That cuts the fibers, so that as you twist the awl, the sharpened edges twist the severed ends out of the way. The birdcage awl, so named because it is used to make holes for bars in wooden birdcages, has a square cross section. Similar to the bradawl, the sharp corners clear the hole as you twist.

ROUGHING OUT CURVES

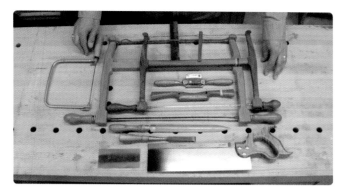

The tools for curved work consist of coping saw, various bow-saws, various spokeshaves, rasp, chisel, scraper and crosscut joinery saw.

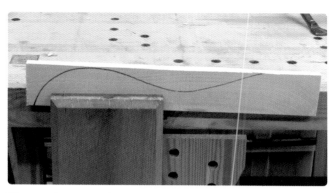

The simplest type of curved work consists of flat workpieces with convex and concave edges. More complex workpieces consist of compound curves.

There are two major strategies for shaping curves. The first uses the most basic of tools: chisels and saws.

The second uses more specialized bowsaws that are able to follow curves. The thin blades are able to turn in the cut. The blades can also be turned in the frames.

1

The simplest method for shaping a convex curve is to use a chisel. Initially you can be very aggressive hogging off large chunks of wood in several passes. Curved work requires creative clamping and support strategies, like the bench hook under this piece. Most clamping setups are oriented toward linear work, with force applied in one direction. For curved work you constantly have to shift the workpiece around as you work on different sections of it. The direction of the grain relative to the tool is constantly changing.

2

As you get close to the line, take finer cuts. Lift the handle to follow the line around as you tap with the mallet. This is a simple form of woodcarving, where the chisel takes a series of small linear cuts that approximate the curve.

3

For portions of the curve that are almost all end grain, take thinner slices. Be careful about chipping off the bottom.

4

To finish off the final end grain section, lay the workpiece down flat and chop or pare across it. Take a series of facets that approximate the curve. Use just the corner of the chisel to slice down small sections.

5

For concave sections, the process is similar, but make vertical stop cuts ahead of where you remove the waste. A stop cut limits how far the waste cut extends, controlling the splitting. Otherwise, the workpiece is liable to continue splitting across the line on the other side of the curve.

6

Make a series of heavy waste cuts closer and closer to the line. Depending on the curve, working bevel down allows you to follow the inside of the curve, just as working bevel up on the convex cut allowed you to follow the outside of the curve.

7

Near the line, take paring cuts. Alternate between bevel up and bevel down as necessary to follow the curve. Make small stop cuts to control the length of the parings.

8

For larger areas, use the crosscut saw to extend the stop cut concept. Make a series of saw cuts that stop just above the line. You can do this on both convex and concave portions. The distance between cuts depends on the wood, its grain characteristics, and the complexity of the curve.

9

With the chisel, start splitting off those sections. They will fracture along the grain between the stop cuts.

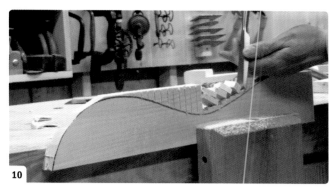

10

After removing a couple of splits from the lowest point, proceed up the slope on one side. Apply force to split in toward the middle, to ensure the fracture doesn't extend into the good wood on the upslope side.

11

Repeat up the other slope, from the lowest to the highest point, splitting the pieces in toward the middle.

12

This leaves a series of small steps that you can easily remove with the chisel. Use it bevel-up to follow convex curves. Always work downhill across the grain, from high spot to low spot. At the very top of a curve, work from the middle out to both sides.

13

Use the chisel bevel-down to follow concave curves. At the very bottom of a curve, work from both sides into the middle. Don't try to work down one side and then back uphill on the other side. On both types of curve, finish up with final hand paring.

14

The completed shape roughed out. Don't worry about the flats and divots. You'll fare all those out with finer tools during fine shaping.

15

A bowsaw can follow curves. Use it with the teeth oriented in the push direction. The cord and toggle for tensioning is known as a Spanish windlass. Wind it up and pluck the saw blade to judge the tension. There should be enough tension to avoid buckling as you push the saw through the wood. Stiffer tension cuts better than loose tension. Always remember to release the tension when you're finished using the saw.

16

When using the saw horizontally, one way to grip it is to hold the handle, with your index finger extended out against the frame for stability. You can use your other hand for added control. As you progress around a curve, turn the blade in the frame so the saw clears the work. With a long blade and smooth, full-length strokes, it cuts quickly.

17

Another grip is to hold it by the frame with your wrist tight against the handle. That provides solid stability and balance. You can wrap your other hand around the frame or around the handle and your wrist. Another way to use the saw is with the work flat on the bench, sawing vertically. In that orientation, hold the saw by the handle, hanging below your hand.

18

This is a smaller bowsaw with a finer blade. It can follow tighter curves, but cuts more slowly.

19

A coping saw is a simple alternative. It also uses a fine blade, and the short length makes it slower. The teeth are oriented for the pull stroke.

20

The completed roughed-out curve. The wavy, wobbly cut line will be faired out with the finer tools.

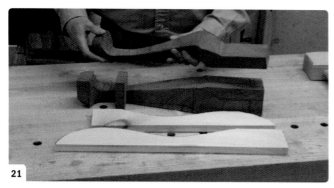

21

These methods work equally well for compound curves, such as cabriole legs. The crude, chunky roughed-out leg on the bench will be refined into graceful, sweeping curves in two dimensions. The block in the middle of the rough leg is for clamping as you work on the different sections.

23

24

To navigate sharp curves such as this V-notch, use the fine bowsaw. For best balance when using this grip, keep the saw upright, with the blade rotated to match the orientation of the cut.

22

Gouges such as these scribing gouges are useful intermediate tools for refining concave curves. They are in-cannel, which means the bevel is on the inside face of the tool. You can also use out-cannel gouges, where the bevel is on the outside. Gouges intended for carving are primarily out-cannel.

To use an in-cannel gouge, stand it up straight near the line. For paring, tuck the handle into your shoulder and push down across the grain with your whole upper body. With heavier gouges, you can use a mallet. Take repeated shavings up to just outside the line, nibbling away at the waste. This leaves a scalloped edge that the fine tools will finish easily. To use an out-cannel gouge, tip it over so the bevel rides vertically down the cut. For convex curves, you can do intermediate shaping with a block plane or a chisel. Adding these intermediate steps allows you to be faster and cruder in the roughing stage, not worrying about trying to get so close to the line.

25

Turn the blade in preparation for a curve, then turn the frame through the curve. Gripping the fame offers firm, positive control to sweep it through the curve. To complete the sharp V in this cut, back out the saw and come in from the other end.

REFINING CURVES

Refining curves is a very sculptural process where you're constantly shifting tools and directions. Spokeshaves excel at this. They are essentially very short-soled planes that are able to follow both convex and concave curves. Hold a spokeshave in a light thumb- and finger-tip grip. Don't hold the handles tight like handlebars. Wrap your fingers loosely around them so they float in your hands. The tool works with both push and pull motions, always working with the grain.

Every spokeshave handles a little differently. For a wooden spokeshave, set the nose of the shave on the work, then roll the tool gently backward until you feel the cutting edge contact it. Control the depth of cut by controlling the roll of the tool as you push or pull it through a curve. Roll it backward off the nose for a heavier cut, forward on the nose for a lighter cut. This takes a little experimentation.

Once you have the desired cut, push smoothly over the curve, rolling the tool through it while maintaining the relative cutting angle. Start at the top of the curve and work down the slope.

For the opposite side, reverse the tool, find the cutting angle, and pull it smoothly. Start at the top of the curve and work down the slope. Skewing the tool to the cut often helps. Concave curves work the same way, from the top down the slope from both sides into the middle. Skewing may help, but may also interfere with following the curve.

For a metal spokeshave, using the same thumb- and finger-tip grip, set the heel of the tool on the work, and roll it forward until the cutting edge contacts. Most metal spokeshaves have an adjustable depth of cut. You can also adjust the iron skewed in the mouth so that it's a fine cut on one end, and a heavy cut on the other end. That forms a continuously varying depth of cut across the width of the iron.

Push down the cut from the top, holding the tool skewed or square across the cut.

Pull down a convex slope into the middle.

Instead of reversing the tool, you can reverse your position. Every piece of wood is different, so you constantly change grip and position. Be sensitive to how the tool responds in your hands as the grain and the curve changes, and adapt as necessary. Let it float in your hands. That's part of what makes these so fun to use.

You can easily chamfer a curve by tipping the spokeshave sideways over the edge. Alternately push and pull to follow the curve around as you maintain the chamfer angle.

The cabinetmaker's rasp is another versatile fine-shaping tool. It's a half-round tool, with one flat side and one rounded side. The teeth are hand-stitched in a random pattern to avoid gouging the surface. This one is a coarse tooth. The pointed tip allows you to get into tighter spaces.

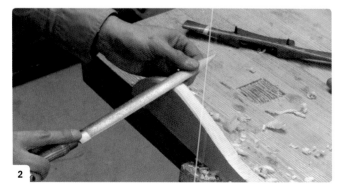

Use the flat side on convex surfaces. Run the tool with a diagonal motion, pushing forward and moving it sideways, always with the grain, using a rolling motion along the curve. You can work at different angles, from directly across the grain, to skewed, to straight along it. Vary the pressure to control the aggressiveness of the cut. Keep it moving around; don't run it over one spot repeatedly or it may dig a divot that spoils the curve. Broad running strokes allow you to fair out a curve.

3 Use the round side on concave surfaces. The motion is the same, a diagonal stroke pushing forward as you move sideways, rolling the tool in the curve.

4 Use the rounded point for detail work, again with a rolling, diagonal motion to avoid divots.

5 The spokeshave leaves a smooth, polished surface, but the rasp leaves a fuzzy surface. Clean that up with a card scraper.

6 In a concave curve, run the scraper down with a scooping motion. At the bottom you can pull it back toward you from the other side. On a convex curve, run it over with a rolling motion that maintains the scraping angle. Scrapers are also good for smoothing out facets left by other tools.

These tools work as a team to quickly clean up lumpy rough cut areas. Switch back and forth as dictated by the curve and the grain. No single tool does all of the work. Run your fingers over the curve to feel for any lumps or rough spots.

Use the point of the rasp in tight, more complex curves. You may only have room for small nibbling work.

Always work "downhill" with the grain. That direction isn't always obvious. The way the work is mounted in the vise, the grain direction, and the way the curve passes over it all dictate the path to follow at each point. Here, sweep the rasp to the left and up the curve as you push it to follow the grain, using a rolling action.

Both the spokeshave and the rasp can perform shaping directly from the flat without any other roughing when you don't need to remove a lot of material. By rolling the spokeshave in from both ends to the middle, you can scoop out a hollow. Conversely, you can roll it over an end to round it. The rasp works similarly, and also allows you to work aggressively across the grain. There you can deliberately form divots to rough it out, then fair them out to the finer shape. The combination of tools provides a lot of flexibility in how you approach the work.

INDEX

B

Bench planes 11, 14
Blind mortise-and-tenon 178, 180-191
Bookmatched joints 127-129
Brace 8, 180, 256-258
    safety 8
Bridle joint 210-214

C

Card scraper 50-56
Chisels 6, 8, 109-121
    safety 8
Coopered joints 129-133
Corner half-lap joints 172-175
Crosscutting 10, 64, 65
Curves 129, 161, 261-269

D

Dados 157-162
Dovetails 215-246
Drawboring 191-194

E

Edge joints 121-123

F

Fillister 137, 140-149
Fine stock preparation 73-91
    length 86-91
    reference edge 79-81
    thicknessing 82-58
    width 82

G

Gang-planing 123-124
Grooves 150-157

H

Half-blind dovetails 215, 241-246
Half-lap joints 162-167
Handplanes 6, 8, 11-15, 70-95
    anatomy 12-14
    safety 8
    types 11-12
Handsaws 8-11, 43-50
    anatomy 8-9
    safety 8
    sharpening 10
    varieties 9-10
Holes 256-260
Hollow grinding 39-42

J

Jigs 5, 16, 20, 34, 39, 43, 97
Joinery 107-175

M

Mallet 8, 109, 115-121
    safety 8
Marking gauges 8, 57-60
Marking knives 8, 62-63
Mortise-and-tenon 176-210

P

Panel raising 98-106
Plane irons 14

R

Rabbets 137-149
Raised panels 98-106
Resawing 64, 68
Ripping 64, 66-67
Rough stock preparation 64-70

S

Safety 8
Saws 6, 8-11, 43-50
    pitch 10
Sharpening
    back preparation 22
    chisels 28, 31, 34, 38, 40
    crosscut saw 48-50
    fine joinery saws 50
    plane irons 25, 30, 32, 35, 42
    ripsaw 48
    saws 43-50
    card scrapers 50-51
Sliding dovetails 246-255
Spring joint 124-126
Squares 57, 61-62
Stropping 21

T

Tapered sliding dovetails 252-255
Tapering 95-97
Through dovetails 218-239
Through mortise-and-tenon 205-209
Tongue-and-groove joints 133-135

W

Wooden planes 14-15
Workbenches 6

Distributed in Canada by Fraser Direct
100 Armstrong Avenue
Georgetown, Ontario L7G 5S4
Canada

Distributed in the U.K. and Europe by
F+W Media International, LTD
Pynes Hill Court
Pynes Hill
Rydon Lane
Exeter
EX2 5SP
Tel: +44 1392 797680

Visit our website at popularwoodworking.com or our consumer website at shopwoodworking.com for more woodworking information.

Other fine Popular Woodworking Books are available from your local bookstore or direct from the publisher.

ISBN-13: 978-1-4403-4890-7

21 20 19 18 17   5 4 3 2 1

Editor: *Scott Francis*
Designer: *Laura Spencer*
Production Coordinator: *Debbie Thomas*

READ THIS IMPORTANT SAFETY NOTICE

To prevent accidents, keep safety in mind while you work. Use the safety guards installed on power equipment. When working on power equipment, keep fingers away from saw blades, wear safety goggles to prevent injuries from flying wood chips and sawdust, wear hearing protection and consider installing a dust vacuum to reduce the amount of airborne sawdust in your woodshop. Don't wear loose clothing or jewelry when working on power equipment. Tie back long hair to prevent it from getting caught in your equipment. People who are sensitive to certain chemicals should check the chemical content of any product before using it. The authors and editors who compiled this book have tried to make the contents as accurate and correct as possible. Plans, illustrations, photographs and text have been carefully checked. All instructions, plans and projects should be carefully read, studied and understood before beginning construction. Due to the variability of local conditions, construction materials, skill levels, etc., neither the author nor Popular Woodworking Books assumes any responsibility for any accidents, injuries, damages or other losses incurred resulting from the material presented in this book. Prices listed for supplies and equipment were current at the time of publication and are subject to change.

METRIC CONVERSION CHART

Inches	Centimeters	2.54
Centimeters	Inches	0.4
Feet	Centimeters	30.5
Centimeters	Feet	0.03
Yards	Meters	0.9
Meters	Yards	1.1

a content + ecommerce company

IDEAS ▪ INSTRUCTION ▪ INSPIRATION

Get downloadable woodworking instruction when you sign up
for our free newsletter at **popularwoodworking.com**.

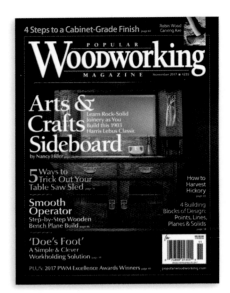

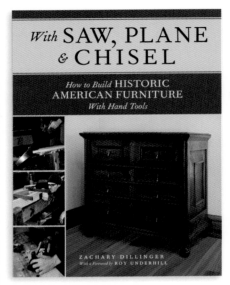

Visit **popularwoodworking.com** to subcribe (look for the red "Subscribe" button on the navigation bar).

These and other great Popular Woodworking products are available at your local bookstore, woodworking store or online supplier. Visit our website at **shopwoodworking.com**.

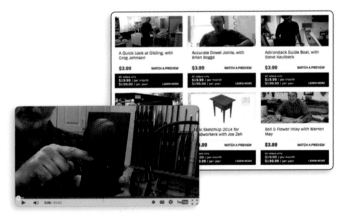

Visit our Website

Find helpful and inspiring articles, videos, blogs, projects and plans at **popularwoodworking.com**.

 For behind the scenes information, become a fan at **Facebook.com/ popularwoodworking**

 For more tips, clips and articles, follow us at **twitter.com/pweditors**

 For visual inspiration, follow us at **pinterest.com/popwoodworking**

 For free videos visit **youtube.com/popularwoodworking**

 Follow us on Instagram **@popularwoodworking**

Popular Woodworking Videos

Subscribe and get immediate access to the web's best woodworking subscription site. You'll find more than 400 hours of woodworking video tutorials and full-length video workshops from world-class instructors on workshops, projects, SketchUp, tools, techniques and more!

videos.popularwoodworking.com